In th[...] I Have Shown You

The Stories of
16 Saints and Christian Heroes
of North America

Jeanne Kun, Editor

the**WORD**
among us

The Word Among Us
9639 Doctor Perry Road
Ijamsville, Maryland 21754
ISBN: 0-932085-83-0
www.wau.org

Cover design by David Crosson

Cover photo of Venerable Pierre Toussaint from Columbia University
Archives—Columbiana Library.

Made and printed in the United States of America

Table of Contents

Introduction

More than three millennia ago, a Semitic herdsman pasturing his flocks around Haran in ancient Mesopotamia embarked on an extraordinarily daring journey of faith. The Lord appeared to Abram and told him, "Go from your country and your kindred and your father's house to the land that I will show you. . . . I will bless you, and make your name great, so that you will be a blessing" (Genesis 12:1-2). Obedient to God's word, Abram set out for the unknown—and became Abraham, the "father of many nations" (17:5). Through his trust in God and God's promises, he also became a timeless model of faith (Romans 4:3,18-22; Galatians 3:6-9).

You are about to meet sixteen men and women who put into action that same bold faith and unquestioning confidence in God. Many left behind family, friends, and the familiarity of their homes in Europe to undertake a perilous journey across the ocean in order to spread the gospel. Others, North American by birth, gave witness to what they believed—often at great risk to themselves—in the young Canadian and American colonies.

But whether born abroad or in the New World, the men and women whose stories are told here willingly embraced God's call to evangelize this vast continent. We think that by reading *In the Land I Have Shown You: The Stories of 16 Saints and Christian Heroes of North*

America, you will be inspired by their unstinting courage, dedication, commitment, and selfless service—all of which so greatly shaped our North American heritage.

The saints as well as the other Christian heroes of North America presented in this collection span the centuries. Their stories are presented chronologically, from the opening era of exploration of the New World to our own day. Not only did these men and women live in different times, their lives reflect a diversity of social and cultural backgrounds as well as vocations and personalities. Here are some of those you will encounter within these pages;

—Marguerite d'Youville of Montreal and Elizabeth Seton of New York, widows who raised children and founded thriving religious congregations.

—Pierre Toussaint, a hairdresser who lived much of his life in slavery.

—Philippine Duchesne and Katharine Drexel, wealthy women who gave to the needy the money they inherited.

—Eusebio Kino, an Italian missionary who, on horse-back, evangelized the native people of the Southwest.

—Henriette Delille, an African American woman from New Orleans who founded a religious order of black nuns to care for the poor.

—Kateri Tekakwitha, who followed a call to become a consecrated virgin in a society where such a choice was unknown.

—Damien de Veuster, who died of leprosy contracted while caring for those exiled to Molokai with that terrible disease.

—Polish-American Jesuit Walter Ciszek, who endured years of imprisonment and hard labor in Siberia and returned "as if from the dead" to continue his priestly ministry in the States.

These lives—each unique and creative—mirror the innumerable ways in which God's Spirit works.

During his papacy, Pope John Paul II has introduced hundreds of new saints to the Church. Those from North America remind Catholics of Canada and the United States that "their own" have also been heroic witnesses to the faith. In the past two decades, the Holy Father has canonized Marguerite Bourgeoys, Philippine Duchesne, Marguerite d'Youville, and Katharine Drexel. In addition, he proclaimed Damien de Veuster, André Bessette, Kateri Tekakwitha, and Francis Xavier Seelos "Blessed," and gave to Pierre Toussaint the title "Venerable." Other North Americans have also been honored by the Church in recent years, but because of the constraints of space, we could not include all of them in this collection.

We are thankful to each of the authors who contributed to *In the Land I Have Shown You*. Their research and hard work have brought to life an important part of our religious and national history. As we read of these heroes, may we be encouraged by their example and draw inspiration to live our lives with the zeal and courage we discover in them.

Jeanne Kun
The Word Among Us

Of Strong Heart

Saint Isaac Jogues
1607 - 1646

by Jeanne Kun

The young Jesuit lay prostrate before the Blessed Sacrament in the mission chapel in New France. As he begged God for the privilege of suffering for the sake of those he sought to bring to Christ, he heard as clear and resonant as speech the following words: "Your prayer has been heard. Be it done to you as you have asked. Be comforted, be of strong heart."

Father Isaac Jogues rejoiced. He believed the words were a prophecy, "issued from the lips of him with whom saying and doing are only one and the same thing." The conviction that God had spoken to him sustained Jogues throughout his ministry, especially during his captivity and torture by the Mohawks. Ultimately, his prayer would be fulfilled with his martyrdom.

Missionary to New France

Isaac Jogues was born into a devout merchant family in Orléans, France, on January 10, 1607. During his boyhood years, Franciscan and Jesuit missionaries were making their first efforts to evangelize the natives in the New World. By the time Isaac entered the Jesuit novitiate in 1624, a Jesuit mission had been established in Huronia (the present province of Ontario). Twelve years of discipline, study, and prayer prepared Isaac well for the life he anticipated as a missionary—though the hardships he would face in the rugged wilderness of New France were far different from his cultured French upbringing. Shortly after his ordination in 1636, the twenty-nine-year-old priest sailed for Quebec with four other Jesuits.

From 1636 until 1642, Father Jogues lived among the natives in Huronia, who named him Ondessonk (bird of prey) because of his keen eye. There, under the tutelage of the veteran missionary Father John de Brébeuf, he learned the language and customs of the Hurons. Together with his fellow missionaries, Jogues suffered from sickness, hunger, and the hardships of the climate. Worse still, Huron sorcerers jealous of the priests' growing influence blamed them for crop failures, poor hunting, or defeats in battle and frequently threatened to kill them. Yet despite all these challenges, some of the Hurons came to profess their belief in the Christian God and accepted baptism.

Under Death's Shadow

In the summer of 1642, while returning in heavily loaded canoes from a journey to Quebec, Ondessonk, his lay assistant and surgeon René Goupil, two other Frenchmen, and almost forty Hurons were ambushed by Mohawks. One of the five nations of the Iroquois, the Mohawks were implacable enemies of the Hurons.

The French and eighteen of the Hurons—many of whom were Christians or catechumens—were taken prisoner. The others were killed or escaped into the woods. In the melee, Ondessonk's canoe capsized, and he lay hidden among the reeds. Rather than flee, he surrendered himself to the Mohawks so that he could accompany his companions and offer whatever help he could in the ordeals sure to follow.

Over the course of the next few weeks, the captives were paraded triumphantly from village to village, made to run the gauntlet, and subjected to hideous torture. The Mohawks pulled out their hair and beards, cut slices of flesh from them—which they roasted and ate—and tore out their fingernails. They also crushed the bones of Ondessonk's forefingers between their teeth and sawed off his left thumb with an oyster shell. At night, the prisoners were tied spread-eagle to the ground, and the children were encouraged to throw live coals on their bare flesh. Many of the Hurons were killed during these ordeals. Goupil was tomahawked to death because he made the sign of the cross over an Indian child. In spite of his own pain, Father Jogues heard his companions' confessions, gave absolution and comfort, and baptized the catechumens. None of them wavered in their new faith.

Love's Labor in Captivity

When the Mohawks' fury abated, they decided to hold Jogues hostage and make him a slave. They forced the "Blackrobe" to do hard tasks and carry heavy loads. They fed him very little, gave him no warm clothing, and constantly threatened to kill him. However, he was adopted into the Wolf clan, and his new "aunt" gave him some measure of freedom to pray alone and to talk with the villagers.

Rather than hating his captors, Ondessonk prayed unceasingly for them and sought to bring as many as possible to salvation. Learning the Mohawks' language, he entered the longhouses—just as he had done among the Hurons—in search of the sick, so that he might win them to Christ before they died. He even nursed the brave who had torn out his fingernails. During his captivity, Ondessonk managed to baptize seventy dying Mohawks. He also consoled and baptized Algonquin and Huron prisoners who were brought into the village for torture and execution.

A Brief Respite

After a year as a slave of the Mohawks, Jogues was taken along to a settlement where the Mohawks traded with the Dutch. There he escaped his captors and remained in hiding for weeks until the Dutch could transport him down the Hudson River to Manhattan Island and on to France, where he landed on Christmas Eve 1643.

Jogues was welcomed as a living martyr by his fellow Jesuits. Queen Anne received him as an honored guest and examined his mangled fingers with tears in her eyes. According to canon law, he could not celebrate Mass with his mutilated hands, but Pope Urban VIII granted Jogues a dispensation. "It would be unjust," he said, "that a martyr for Christ should not drink the blood of Christ."

A humble man, Jogues was distressed by these honors and longed to be back among the Indians. In the spring of 1644, after only a three-month stay in his own country, Jogues' superiors allowed him to return to New France.

Mission of Peace

In the year after Jogues' return, the Iroquois and French began to negotiate a peace treaty. Governor Montmagny asked him to be an ambassador representing the French. As the Jesuit understood the Mohawk language and the Iroquois knew of his high standing among the French, there could be no better peace envoy. Jogues readily agreed, though this meant returning to Ossernenon (near present-day Auriesville, New York), the Mohawk village where he had been tortured and enslaved.

Jogues and his companions reached Ossernenon in June 1646. A great multitude gathered to see the party, and those who had once made life so miserable for him now pretended to have forgotten their past deeds and greeted him cordially. An assembly of the chiefs was held, benevolent speeches were given promising peace, and furs and belts of wampum were exchanged.

The council ended favorably, and Jogues again began to administer the sacraments to Christian captives and to baptize the dying. The mission of diplomacy completed, the peace envoy returned to Quebec, but Jogues left a chest containing Mass supplies and personal effects in Ossernenon, hoping to return the next season. He showed the box and its contents to the villagers, assured them there was nothing harmful in it, and entrusted it to them.

Espoused in Blood

Though eager to establish a Mohawk mission, Isaac and his superiors were cautious. Not long afterward, however, conditions seemed favorable, and it was decided that Ondessonk should winter among the Iroquois. He wrote to a friend in France:

> My heart tells me that if I have the happiness of being employed in this mission, *Ibo et non redibo* [I shall go never to return]; but I shall be happy if our Lord will complete the sacrifice where he has begun it, and make the little blood I have shed in that land the pledge of what I would give from every vein of my body and my heart. In a word, this people is "a bloody spouse to me"—"In my blood have I espoused it to me" [Exodus 4:25]. May our good Master who has purchased them in his blood, open to them the door of his gospel, as well as to the four allied nations near them. Adieu, dear Father; pray to him to unite me inseparably to him.

On September 24, Jogues left Quebec for his third journey to the Five Nations, accompanied by a dedicated lay missionary, John de Lalande, and some Huron companions. As they approached Ossernenon, the group was attacked by a war party from the village and taken captive. Jogues reminded the Mohawks of their invitation for him to return and of the treaty, but to no avail. They angrily accused the Blackrobe of having put a curse on them— they had experienced a scourge of disease and a plague of worms that destroyed their crops—and they blamed the chest he had left among them for their misfortunes. Jogues' "adoptive" Wolf clan defended him, and the chiefs' council honored the treaty and let him live. The Bear clan, however, decided to kill Ondessonk on their own.

On the evening of October 18, 1646, Jogues was invited to a feast in one of the Mohawk longhouses. As he stooped to enter through the low door, the brave following behind him split his skull with a tomahawk. The traitors immediately cut off his head and displayed it on the palisades of the village. The next day, they killed John de Lalande and the Hurons. News of the martyrdoms did not reach Quebec until June 1647.

A Harvest of Souls

The Iroquois broke the treaty with the French and, in the following years, mercilessly attacked the Hurons. They destroyed all their villages and the Jesuit mission posts among them. Fathers John de Brébeuf, Gabriel Lalemant, Charles Garnier, Anthony Daniel, and Noel Charbanel were martyred in Huronia between July 4, 1648, and December 8, 1649. Within months after these martyrdoms, fourteen hundred Hurons were converted to Christ. The seed of faith was watered by the blood of these martyrs, and an abundance of souls harvested for heaven.

The brave who tomahawked Jogues and another who had been wounded attempting to deflect the blow from the victim were later converted to Christianity. The murderer took "Isaac" as his baptismal name and died repentant, satisfied that he was going to heaven.

Ten years after Jogues was martyred in Ossernenon, Kateri Tekakwitha was born in the same village. She became a witness to Christ through the undaunted efforts of the Jesuits who followed the first North American martyrs. The first Native American to be beatified, Kateri is among the fruits for whom Isaac Jogues shed his blood in the hopes that his holocaust would hasten the conversion of the Mohawks.

The eight North American martyrs—René Goupil, John de Lalande, and Fathers Isaac Jogues, John de Brébeuf, Gabriel Lalemant, Charles Garnier, Anthony Daniel, and Noel Charbanel—were canonized by Pope Pius XI in 1930.

Of Strong Heart

This selection is from a lengthy narrative about his captivity written by Father Isaac Jogues while he was under the protection of Dutch colonists in Renssalaerswyck (present-day Albany). He addressed the letter, dated August 5, 1643, to the Provincial of the Jesuits in Paris.

Raising a joyful shout, which made the forest ring, "as conquerors who rejoice after taking a prey" [Isaiah 9:3], they bore us off, as captives towards their own land. We were twenty-two; three had been killed. By the favor of God our sufferings on that march, which lasted thirteen days, were indeed great; hunger and heat and menaces, the savage fury of the Indians, the intense pain of our untended and now putrifying wounds, which actually swarmed with worms. No trial, however, came harder upon me than to see them after five or six days approach us jaded with the march, and, in cold blood, with minds in nowise excited by passion, pluck out our hair and beard and drive their nails, which were always very sharp, deep into parts most tender and sensitive to the slightest impression.

But this was outward; my internal sufferings affected me still more, when I beheld that funeral procession of doomed Christians pass before my eyes, among them five old converts, the main pillars of the infant Huron Church. Indeed I ingenuously admit that I was again and again unable to withhold my tears, mourning over their lot and that of my other companions, and full of anxious solicitude for the future. For I beheld the way to the Christian faith closed by these Iroquois on the Hurons and countless other nations, unless they were checked by some seasonable dispensation of Divine Providence.

On the eighth day we fell in with a troop of two hundred Indians going out to fight; and as it is the custom for savages when out on war parties to initiate themselves, as it were, by cruelty, under the belief that their success will be greater as they shall have been more cruel, they thus received us. First rendering thanks to the Sun, which they imagine presides over war, they congratulated their countrymen by a joyful volley of musketry. Each then cut some stout clubs in the neighboring wood in order to receive us. After we had landed from the canoes they fell upon us from both sides with their clubs in such fury, that I, who was the last and therefore most exposed to their blows, sank overcome by their number and severity, before I had accomplished half the rocky way that led to the hill on which a stage had been erected for us. I thought I should soon die there; and so, partly because I could not, partly because I cared not, I did not arise.

How long they spent their fury on me he knows, for whose love and sake it is delightful and glorious thus to suffer. Moved at length by a cruel mercy, and wishing to carry me to their country alive, they ceased to strike. And thus half dead and drenched in blood, they bore me to the scaffold. Here I had scarce begun to breathe when they ordered me to come down to load me with scoffs and insults, and countless blows on my head and shoulders, and indeed on my whole body. I should be tedious were I to attempt to tell of all that the French prisoners suffered. They burnt one of my fingers, and crunched another with their teeth; others already thus mangled they so wrenched by the tattered nerves, that even now, though healed, they are frightfully deformed. Nor indeed was the lot of my fellow-sufferers much better. . . .

At last, on the eve of the Assumption of the Blessed Virgin, we reached the first village of the Iroquois. I thank our Lord Jesus Christ that on the day when the whole Christian world exults in the glory of his mother's Assumption into heaven, he called us to some small share and fellowship of his sufferings and cross. Indeed we had, during the journey, always foreseen that it would be a sad and bitter day for us. It would have been easy for René and me to escape that day and the flames, for being often unbound and at a distance from our guards, we might, in the darkness of night, have struck off from the road, and even though we should never reach our countrymen, we would at least meet a less cruel death in the woods. He constantly refused to do this, and I was resolved to suffer all that could befall me, rather than forsake in death Frenchmen and Christian Hurons, depriving them of the consolation which a priest can afford. ⟻⊚⟾

The Life of Isaac Jogues

1607 - Born and baptized on January 10 in Orléans, France

1624 - Enters the Jesuit novitiate in Rouen

1636 - Ordained in January; sails for New France in April and reaches Ihonotiria, a Huron village located on the northernmost point of the Huron peninsula, on September 16

1642 - Jogues and his companions are ambushed and captured by Mohawks in early August, and are paraded from village to village and tortured for several weeks; René Goupil is martyred on September 29

1643 - Escapes after a year of being held as a slave-hostage and, with the help of the Dutch, reaches France on Christmas Eve

1644 - Arrives back in Quebec, to the joy and surprise of his fellow Jesuits who had not received news of his escape from the Mohawks

1645 - Hopes are enkindled for negotiating a peace treaty between the French and the Iroquois

1646 - Jogues sets out on May 16 for Ossernenon as the French peace ambassador; completes the diplomatic mission successfully and arrives back in Quebec on July 3; sets out on September 24 on his last venture to the Mohawks; tomahawked to death on October 18

1647 - News of Father Isaac Jogues' martyrdom reaches Quebec in June

1930 - Pope Pius XI canonizes the North American martyrs on June 29; their feast day is celebrated on October 19

In the Land I Have Shown You

Pioneer in the City of Mary

Saint Marguerite Bourgeoys
1620 - 1700

by Jeanne Kun

Ville-Marie—the "City of Mary"—was situated at the foot of the rocky eminence the French explorer Jacques Cartier had named Mount Royal. From the edge of this vast Canadian wilderness, Marguerite Bourgeoys could look back on her long and venturesome life in Ville-Marie and know that she had truly been guided there by the Blessed Virgin.

Marguerite Bourgeoys was affectionately known by all in Ville-Marie as the "Mother of the Colony." For forty-six years, she had endured the rigors of poverty, Indian attacks, rustic lodgings, plague, and food shortages side by side with her neighbors as they faced the challenge of making a home in New France. But she was more than just a pioneer in the settlement. She was also a pioneer in education and in religious life. She opened the first school in Ville-Marie and founded the first non-cloistered teaching order to be established in Canada. As Mary had journeyed to her cousin Elizabeth, Marguerite had journeyed to the New World to bring Christ's love to others.

Searching for God's Way

Marguerite spent the first thirty-three years of her life in Troyes, France, far from the island in the St. Lawrence River where she would be buried. Born in 1620, the seventh child of thirteen in the family of Abraham and Guillemette Bourgeoys, she enjoyed a healthy and happy home life. By her own report, she was popular with the other girls in Troyes, "frivolous," and enjoyed dressing fashionably.

All this changed, however, when, at twenty years old, she experienced an inner transformation. While she was participating in a procession in honor of Our Lady of the Rosary, Marguerite passed a church with a statue of the Blessed Virgin standing above its portal. "Glancing up to look at it," she later wrote, "I found it very beautiful. At the same time, I found myself so moved and so changed that I no longer recognized myself. When I returned home, this was apparent to everyone."

Marguerite's future was shaped by her response to this experience. First she went to confession. Then she gave up her "pretty clothes" and joined a lay group of women associated with the cloistered Notre Dame Sisters in Troyes. These young women dressed simply, prayed together, and reached out to the poor. With her warm and loving personality, Marguerite was a natural leader and was soon chosen president of the association. But when she sought to enter a Carmelite convent, she was surprisingly rejected. After she was also turned down by another order of nuns, her spiritual director, Father Antoine de Gendret, suggested that God might instead be calling her to a more active ministry.

For hundreds of years, women religious had lived a strictly enclosed life. But in seventeenth-century France, innovative groups were forming that sought to care for the poor and sick outside the confines of the cloister. These new religious communities—among them the Visitation Sisters founded by Sts. Francis de Sales and Jane de Chantal—were seeking approval from the traditionally minded hierarchy of the Church. Recognizing the merits of this fresh expression of religious life, Gendret wrote a provisional rule for Marguerite and encouraged her to begin a non-cloistered institute with two friends.

Inspired by Mary's visit to her cousin Elizabeth, Marguerite and her companions identified their new venture with "the journeying Virgin Mary," who cared for those around her. They wanted to lead the kind of life they believed Jesus' mother had lived during her days on earth. Their effort failed after a few years, however, when one of the women died and the other decided to marry. Left alone, Marguerite wondered what God now intended for her.

A New World Opens

Not long after this, Paul de Chomedey de Maisonneuve, the governor of Ville-Marie, visited his sister, who was a cloistered Notre Dame nun in Troyes. He told her of the colony's need for a schoolteacher, and she recommended her friend Marguerite.

Ville-Marie had been founded in 1642 under the auspices of the Associates of the Montreal Company, a group of French men and women interested in establishing a colony in New France based on the ideals of the early Christian community described in the Acts of the Apostles. They also hoped that such a witness would attract the Huron, Algonquin, and Iroquois Indians to Christ. Advantageously located on the St. Lawrence River, Ville-Marie—later called Montreal—would, during French Canada's adventurous history, become the head of the country and a "voyageur" terminal for missionaries, soldiers, traders, and explorers. But in 1653 when Marguerite prayerfully considered de Maisonneuve's invitation, the colony was still quite primitive.

Gendret encouraged Marguerite, who was then thirty-three years old, to go to New France. She also received remarkable spiritual guidance: "One morning when I was wide awake, a tall woman in a white gown said to me distinctly: 'Go, I shall not forsake you'; and I felt that it was the Blessed Virgin although I did not see her face. This gave me the greatest assurance for the voyage; nothing seemed difficult any more." Again Mary played a decisive role in Marguerite's life, and the memory of this vision encouraged her through many years of hardship in Canada.

Life in the City of Mary

When Marguerite arrived in Ville-Marie, all the colonists were being sheltered in a fort that enclosed their common lodgings, chapel, soldiers' garrison, hospital, and storage buildings. The total population of the settlement was 196, which included only fourteen women and the reinforcement of the one hundred men she had sailed with. Very few children had been born or survived since the colony's beginnings, so Marguerite had no students as yet. So, with her practical nature and organizational skills, she managed the governor's household where she boarded with other colonists and gladly took on any work that was helpful to the colony.

Not long after her arrival, Marguerite rallied the settlers to restore a large wooden cross that de Maisonneuve had raised in the forest when Ville-Marie was first established. At the site where the original cross had been burned by the Iroquois, they found the remains of a banner that had been given to the governor by his sister in Troyes. The words on the banner were still legible: "Holy Mother of God, pure Virgin with a royal heart, keep for us a place in your Montreal." This discovery was important to Marguerite, for she saw in it another confirmation from Mary of her vocation in New France.

Five years later, Marguerite opened Ville-Marie's first school in a renovated stone stable. Eight names—three girls and five boys—appeared on the register dated April 30, 1658. "Sister" Bourgeoys, as the colonists by now called her, knew that reading and writing were essential for the children to make their way in life. But she also knew the challenges of being a pioneer firsthand, so she included in her lessons the practical skills vitally related to sustaining life in the wilderness.

In addition to her students, Marguerite took under her wing young women who came from France to marry. She taught them the essentials of housekeeping and instructed them in the responsibilities that awaited them as wives and mothers. She used the domestic life of Mary as a model of inspiration for these prospective brides. She also prepared children for their First Communion, consoled wives widowed by Indian attacks and parents whose children died, and even cared for several Iroquois babies she adopted as her own.

A Dream Fulfilled

Soon Marguerite needed more teachers—and she still cherished the hope of establishing a non-cloistered order of women. Such a community would be able to serve wherever there was need in the colony. So she sailed for France, where she recruited four women to join her as teachers and also proposed to them her idea of forming a sisterhood. During their ocean voyage in July 1659, the little group began their community. They lived, prayed, ate, and slept literally side by side with those they came to serve.

After Marguerite brought her companions to the stable school, it was looked upon as a convent and house of prayer—even though the women wore no religious habit and had not yet taken any formal vows. The provisional rule they followed at this time was very simple. During the day they ran the school and taught domestic skills to the girls preparing for marriage. At night they did mending and laundry for the men of Ville-Marie (who still far outnumbered the women) in exchange for their services as carpenters, stonemasons, and ironsmiths. The sisters' tumultuous lives were lived in a single room, the ground floor of the stable where a fireplace had been installed.

The loft comprised their sleeping area. They had absolutely no privacy, not even in the forest outside. In the 1660s it was still too perilous to leave the fort alone.

As the years progressed, Ville-Marie grew and so did the fledgling sisterhood. In 1667 the colonists petitioned King Louis XIV to grant a civil charter to Marguerite's community, and in 1669 Bishop François de Montmorency Laval authorized the women to teach throughout the diocese. Marguerite sailed again for France in 1670 and returned with nine new volunteers. In 1676 the Congregation of Notre Dame of Montreal was canonically erected by Laval as a "Community of the Church." Daughters of the first colonists—young women whom Marguerite had known from birth—began to join the sisters. With her wide heart and typical open-mindedness, Marguerite also received Iroquois women into the community.

Marguerite's Legacy

Year by year, the Congregation matured and its ministry spread. New schools were opened throughout the region, including a mission school for the Iroquois. The community also knew sorrow. Fire destroyed their convent in 1683, and two sisters died, one of them Marguerite's niece who had come from France to join her work. When Mother Bourgeoys resigned as superior in 1693 because of her advancing age, Marie Barbier, the first child of Ville-Marie to have joined the Congregation, was elected to succeed her. Finally, in 1698, Bishop de Saint-Vallier, Laval's successor, approved the rule fully embodying the community's ideals, and Marguerite and her sisters publicly pronounced their religious vows.

Late in 1699, in a generous act of love, Marguerite prayed that God would take her life in the place of the critically ill young novice mistress. Her prayer was answered: The nun recovered, and Marguerite died on January 12, 1700, when she was seventy-nine years old.

Mother Bourgeoys was canonized by Pope John Paul II in 1982. Today, the Congregation she founded numbers fifteen hundred sisters. In nine countries around the world they teach in schools of every level, offer hospitality to the homeless, and care for the sick and destitute, continuing to live out Marguerite's vision of "the journeying Virgin Mary."

Mother Bourgeoys occasionally recorded her thoughts on the providence of the Eternal Father, the example of the Blessed Virgin, the spiritual life, and her Congregation. The following reflections are from her undated notes.

I compare this Community to a square in a large garden. For all Christendom is a great garden created by God and all the communities are as so many plots in this large garden. Ours, as small as it is, does not fail to be one of those little squares the Gardener has kept for himself to set out a number of plants and flowers. In this little garden, they are all different in color, in savor, in fragrance. The Gardener takes great care to fertilize and enrich this earth and to clear it. He takes care of all the seeds he wishes to sow and bring to growth there, so that they may not take up his ground if they have any vices and so that they may not be choked by weeds. This is why he does not fail to come back over this land and to water it at need. When he discovers that some of these plants do not profit from his care, or that they are misshapen, he pulls them up to make room for others.

The sisters of the Congregation are as so many plants which occupy one of these squares in the garden, that is to say, the Community. Before being received, they are cleansed by a general confession and by the other attentions that are given them to detach them from all that can prevent them from growing in virtue. They are purified once or twice a week by confession, nourished and enriched on Sundays and several other days each week by Holy Communion, watered continually by the rain and waters of heavenly grace, good reading, and instructions; proved from time to time by the fire of tribulation, of contempt, of illness, of contradiction, of mortifications and other trials. If after all this care, the sisters do not advance in virtue, if they let themselves be dominated by bad habits, how that will displease the Master of the garden! And what will be their fate in the end, if not to be pulled up as barren plants which have a rank odor?

Let us work then to cultivate flowers and fruits worthy to be presented to him through the hands of the Blessed Virgin, our dear Mother, our worthy teacher, and first superior. If we put our minds to this, we will find no difficulty in poor and humiliating tasks, in following the way of perfection, and in having God present in everything we do so as to please him alone.

The Life of Marguerite Bourgeoys

1620 - Born and baptized on April 17 in Troyes, France

1642 - The colony of Ville-Marie is founded by Monsieur Paul de Chomedey de Maisonneuve under the auspices of the Associates of the Montreal Company of Paris

1653 - Marguerite arrives in Ville-Marie on November 16

1658 - Opens the first school in Ville-Marie in a renovated stone stable on April 30; later in the year departs for France to recruit teachers

1659 - Returns from France with her first four companions

1667 - The residents of Ville-Marie petition King Louis XIV for a civil charter for Marguerite's institute

1669 - Bishop François de Montmorency Laval authorizes the sisters to teach throughout the territory

1672 - Marguerite returns from another voyage to France with additional volunteers

1676 - Bishop Laval approves Marguerite's institute on August 6, formally constituting the Congregation of Notre Dame of Montreal as a "Community of the Church"

1698 - The Congregation accepts the final revision of the rule as approved by Bishop de Saint-Vallier, successor to Bishop Laval, on June 24; the sisters make their first public pronouncement of vows on June 25

1700 - Marguerite dies on January 12

1950 - Beatified by Pope Pius XII on November 12

1982 - Canonized by Pope John Paul II on October 31; her feast day is January 12

The "Cowboy Saint"

Eusebio Kino
1645 - 1711

by Louise Perrotta

T he Indian warriors appeared suddenly one Tuesday in April 1683, near a palm grove on the southeast coast of the California peninsula. Hostility was in the air as they advanced toward the party of Spaniards who were clearing brush and cutting timber for a pioneer mission.

Spotting the Guiacuros' bows and arrows, Governor Atondo and his soldiers picked up their weapons. They anticipated trouble. Standing nearby, Eusebio Francisco Kino, S.J., reacted differently. He anticipated an evangelistic opportunity—one he had been seeking for two decades. With a disarming smile, the Blackrobe moved forward to meet the first of the many Native Americans he would come to know during his labors on the California-Sonora-Arizona frontier.

It was the first step in an extraordinary missionary career. Over the next twenty-eight years, Padre Kino's latent gifts exploded in a dazzling array of activities and accomplishments. In the words of his main biographer, Herbert Bolton, this dauntless and visionary "padre on horseback" emerged as "the most picturesque missionary pioneer of all North America—explorer, astronomer, cartographer, mission builder, ranchman, cattle king, and defender of the frontier."

Delayed Action

Eusebio Kino was thirty-seven when he first set foot in California. His missionary zeal, ignited when he was eighteen, had burned ever since. Afflicted with a life-threatening illness, the young man had made a solemn vow that determined the direction of his life. He promised his patron saint, Francis Xavier, that if he recovered, he would enter the Society of Jesus and offer himself as a missionary to China.

China was worlds away from Segno, Italy, the Tyrolean Alpine village where Eusebio grew up. However, he was captivated by the exciting stories he heard from his parents, Francisco and Margherita, about a priest relative who worked in the Chinese missions. Like Francis Xavier before him, Eusebio started dreaming of Far East evangelism.

Following his recovery, Kino entered the Society of Jesus and began its twelve-year formation, studying and teaching throughout southern Germany. He lived in Bavaria so long that he joked, "I am in doubt whether I should call myself an Italian or a German!"

But China was always on Eusebio's mind. He preferred living in rooms with east-facing windows—"so that I might be comforted many times during the day, by the mere sight of the East." Knowing that Chinese rulers especially respected the mathematical sciences, he studied them diligently. He became proficient at mapmaking and astronomy. When the "Great Comet" of 1680 appeared, he made observations and published them in a book that combined dubious conjectures about the comet's "ominous import" with what one reviewer called "perfect knowledge" of the sciences.

In 1670, Kino asked his superiors to select him for a foreign mission, preferably China. After eight years and seven more letters of request, he finally got a yes. He would go to either Asia or America, where Jesuits were attending to the spiritual needs of Spain's spreading empire. The choice was left up to him and another Jesuit who had also been tapped for missionary work. They decided to settle the issue by drawing lots.

"Mexico," read the slip of paper that Eusebio drew. Disappointed but eager to evangelize, he prayed for grace—and kept hoping for China.

Detours and Dead Ends
Was the New World God's last word? The new missionary must have wondered. Everything that could go wrong did go wrong. He arrived at the Spanish port of Cádiz, his point of embarkation for the Americas, only to see the "melancholy spectacle" of the fleet sailing away. Finding passage on another ship was difficult; the one he finally boarded went aground and had to be abandoned almost immediately. Wet and stripped of baggage, Kino returned to port, waited some more, and worked on his Spanish. These events provided a hard lesson in patience: In all, the journey from Germany to Mexico took almost three years.

It was also a time for learning to discern God's will. Were these obstacles simply tests along the way to America, or did they indicate that the China door might open after all? Both an influential Spanish duchess and a Jesuit director of missions for the Orient were making efforts to get Eusebio's marching orders revised. He struggled to be impartial: "I dare not anticipate, seek, or desire one place rather than another lest someone should rebuke me with the words, 'You know not what you ask.'"

With the question unresolved as he reached Mexico in May 1681, Kino entrusted the outcome to Our Lady of Guadalupe. Before long, he had his answer. The Spanish king had authorized an expedition to Baja California—an area Spain had been trying unsuccessfully to colonize and evangelize for a century and a half. Eusebio would accompany the expedition as missionary and official mapmaker. God had spoken. With a prayer that God's will be done, Eusebio shelved his China dreams and plunged wholeheartedly into this new adventure.

California or Bust?

The California mission lasted a little less than three years. Two attempts to establish settlements failed—doomed by drought, epidemic, lack of funds, and local hostility provoked by the military's acts of aggression. Through it all, Padre Kino remained optimistic. Focused on "fishing for the best, the divine, the celestial pearls, which are souls," he contended that the native peoples of California were basically "gentle, affable, peaceful, extremely friendly, loving and lovable" and that "many of them were begging for holy baptism."

Finally, however, despite his anguished protests, the California venture was terminated. By March 1687, Kino was beginning a new assignment as missionary to the Pimería Alta, the area that includes present-day northern Sonora, Mexico, and southern Arizona. At forty-two, he had finally arrived in the region where he would labor for the rest of his life.

Though it was short-lived, Eusebio's California experience had given him the chance to experiment with the missionary approach he would use as "Apostle to the Pima Indians." It was a type of friendship evangelism conducted through gestures and sign language. Little gifts were offered—glass beads, ribbons, mirrors, scissors—and the recipients followed suit. Kino delightedly noted the development in his diary: "We now began to be very friendly and familiar, and they gave us roasted mescal cactus heads, which were very good, little nets very well made, and feathers of birds which they wore on their heads. We showed them a crucifix, and next day a statue of Our Lady of Guadalupe."

Two days later, he was teaching his new friends to make "the sign of the Holy Cross," with hopes that "within a few months we may be able to baptize." Except for infants and those in danger of death, no Native Americans were baptized unless they had received some religious instruction and lived near a mission where they could continue it.

Learning to Evangelize

Since sign language went only so far, Eusebio decided to learn the local languages. At his very first encounter with the Guiacuros, he and a fellow Jesuit walked around "with inkwell in their hands," taking notes on vocabulary and pronunciation. In time, Kino mastered numerous tribal languages and compiled several vocabularies. He made friends with the children, who were especially good teachers, and discovered ingenious ways to communicate the basics of the faith. In one classic example, he explained the Resurrection by reviving some dead-looking flies!

The Indians, too, studied a new language. Beginning with Spanish words like *Jesús* and *María,* they progressed to the Our Father, Hail Mary, Credo, and Ten Commandments. Some absorbed a great deal of Spanish. In his historical journal, *Celestial Favors,* Kino marveled at one warrior who greeted his traveling party with the impressive salutation: "Blessed and exalted be the Most Holy Sacrament of the altar and the immaculate conception of Most Holy Mary." This feat was "a source of some wonder to us," the missionary noted.

Padre Kino used the rich vestments and ornaments of religious ceremonies to attract the native peoples and pique their curiosity. However, like parents of large families who struggle to conduct reverent prayer around the dinner table, he learned to approach such occasions with flexibility and a sense of humor. With relish, he described how one Mass degenerated into a near riot when a dog, teased by a boy, retaliated by biting someone.

On another occasion, a group who had come for a religious ceremony became frightened at what Eusebio thought was "a large and pretty statue of the Holy Christ"—the crucified Christ, no doubt—for as soon as they saw it, they ran away, terrified. "They hardly dared to talk with us, or among themselves except in very low tones or in whispers, asking who that person was and who had killed him, and if he were some cruel enemy of ours, for it worried them very greatly to think that we treated people so."

Eusebio's reassuring ways and burning love of God broke through every barrier. By his gentle approach and attractive personality, he won the people's trust. By his genuine love and respect, he won their hearts.

Father of Missions

In March 1687, after a fifteen hundred-mile horseback journey from Mexico City, Padre Kino arrived at the frontier mission station of Cucurpe on Sonora's upper San Miguel River. To the east and south were Spanish settlements— silver mining camps and towns, ranches, and missions. North and west lay Pimería Alta, the little-known country of the Upper Pima tribes.

As if making up for lost time, Kino quickly scouted out his new territory. He delighted in every canyon, cottonwood grove, and mountain pass he traveled through. Even more, he rejoiced in the receptive spirit of the country's inhabitants, elated that "in all places, they received with love the word of God for the sake of their eternal salvation." By week's end, he had visited a seventy-five-mile area and established missions in four tribal villages. Nuestra Señora de los Dolores (Our Lady of Sorrows), the first in the chain of more than twenty missions he founded during the next quarter century, became his home base.

From Dolores, Padre Kino pushed the frontier of missionary work and exploration. He rode through wilderness inhabited by potentially hostile tribes, opening trails and often averaging thirty miles a day for weeks or months at a stretch. A careful observer, he wrote journals, letters, and a memoir that are important sources for the history of Sonora and Arizona. He was the first to traverse and accurately map these regions, as well as Mexican California, which he conclusively proved was not an island as many thought, but the lower (*baja*) part of a large land mass.

Eusebio, however, was first and foremost a missionary who thrilled at discovering unknown lands because he saw them as fields ripe for Christ. His explorations took place in the context of itinerant missions, where he took the gospel to new tribes and encouraged them to link up with the mission towns he was establishing.

Among all of Kino's missions, Dolores stood out as his crowning achievement. By 1695, it included more than ninety families and was a self-sustaining center of religious life and economic activity. Eusebio pointed with pride to its church—simple but "adequately furnished with ornaments, chalices, cups of gold, bells, and choir chapel"—and its rectory, carpenter shop, blacksmith forge, and water mill.

Concerned about providing food and economic independence for the converts who came to live at his missions, Padre Kino was resourceful and innovative. He introduced cattle and established the beginnings of ranching; he was "easily the cattle king of his day and region," according to one biographer. He helped the people to expand their farming skills by teaching them to grow wheat and cultivate imported fruits and vegetables. "He fashioned a whole new economy in the harsh, sun-baked land," one Arizona historian wrote. None of this industry was for personal gain. As a Jesuit coworker observed, Eusebio "never had more than two coarse shirts, because he gave everything as alms to the Indians."

Earthly and Heavenly Kingdoms

Padre Kino was a diplomat walking a fine line between frequently conflicting forces. On the one hand, he supported the Spanish king and viewed the expansion of the empire as a grand opportunity to spread Christianity. On the other hand, his overriding loyalty to the King of Kings put him at odds with any Spaniard who failed to treat the indigenous people with respect.

Mine owners and others looking to exploit the Native Americans' goods or labor had to contend with the fearless Jesuit, who adamantly enforced royal decrees outlawing such abuses. When ruthless soldiers threatened to take innocent lives, Eusebio intervened. Once, hearing that a Pima man was to be executed the next day, he made a perilous seventy-five-mile journey at night to rescue him. In April 1695, following an uprising that left several missions destroyed and another Jesuit martyred, Kino stepped in as a peacemaker to avert further bloodshed and correct the abuses that had provoked the revolt in the first place.

Often, Eusebio defended the Pimas against false accusations that they were too hostile and insignificant to evangelize. Regrettably, some attacks came from his own superior, who envied Kino's success and wrote a lengthy exposé to discredit him. A higher-placed Jesuit wrote to Eusebio and declared himself "greatly grieved" by this persecution and struck by "your patience and virtue."

Padre Kino's virtue was in evidence as he made his final approach to the heavenly kingdom he had served so energetically. On March 15, 1711, while celebrating the inaugural Mass in a new mission chapel dedicated to his beloved St. Francis Xavier, the sixty-six-year-old missionary felt ill. He died before midnight—"as he had lived, with extreme humility and poverty," wrote his friend and successor, Padre Luís Velarde. "His death bed, as his bed had always been, consisted of two calf-skins for a mattress, two blankets such as the Indians use for covers, and a pack saddle for a pillow."

Padre Kino was buried "on the gospel side" of the chapel in Magdalena, Sonora, Mexico. His gravesite was rediscovered on May 21, 1966, and has become a popular pilgrimage destination. Fittingly enough, Eusebio shares the honors with St. Francis Xavier, whose intercession he had relied on his entire life.

Today, many of Eusebio's admirers are asking his favorite saint to intercede for one more intention on his behalf: the successful completion of Kino's beatification process. When that prayer becomes reality, the intrepid "padre on horseback" will become the Church's first cowboy saint.

The "Cowboy Saint"

This selection is taken from an account
Eusebio Kino wrote of his expedition into
Arizona, where the Sobaípuri tribe had asked
him to send missionaries. In 1692 he established a mission dedicated to St. Francis
Xavier at the Sobaípuris' town of Bac. Today
the majority of the Sobaípuris' descendants—
the Tohono O'odham tribe, which includes
23,000 members living throughout southern
Arizona—are Catholics. San Xavier del Bac,
just southwest of Tucson, is a lively parish
staffed by Franciscan friars.

T he Sobaípuris came to meet us, some with crosses,
which they gave us, kneeling with great veneration,
and asking us on behalf of all their people to go to
their *rancherías* [villages] also. The father visitor said to me
that those crosses which they carried were tongues that
spoke volumes and with great force, and that we could not
fail to go where by means of them they called us. . . .

In spite of the obstacles which were present, and seeing
that the whole of Pimería was quiet, during the last part of
August and the first part of September 1692, I went in,
with fifty pack animals, my servants, and some native officials, to the Sobaípuris. . . . I found the natives very affable
and friendly, and particularly so in the principal *ranchería*
of San Xavier del Bac, which contains more than eight
hundred souls.

I spoke to them of the word of God, and on a map of the world showed them the lands, the rivers, and the seas over which we fathers had come from afar to bring them the saving knowledge of our holy faith. And I told them also how in ancient times the Spaniards were not Christians, how Santiago [St. James the Apostle] came to teach them the faith, and how for the first fourteen years he was able to baptize only a few, because of which the most holy apostle was discouraged, but that the most holy Virgin appeared to him and consoled him, telling him that the Spaniards would convert the rest of the peoples of the world.

And I showed them on the map of the world how the Spaniards and the faith had come by sea to Vera Cruz, and had gone in to Puebla and to Mexico, Guadalajara, Sinaloa, and Sonora, and now to Nuestra Señora de los Dolores in the land of the Pimas, where there were already many persons baptized, a house, church, bells, and images of saints, plentiful supplies, wheat, maize, and many cattle and horses. I told them that they could go and see it all, and even ask about it right away of the Indians who were with me. They listened with pleasure to these and other talks concerning God, heaven, and hell, and told me that they wished to be Christians, and gave me some infants to baptize.

The Life of Eusebio Kino

1645 - Born and baptized in the Alpine village of Segno, Italy, on August 10

1663 - Vows to become a Jesuit missionary, pending recovery from a life-threatening illness

1665 - Begins Jesuits' twelve-year training program on November 20

1678 - Receives long-awaited missionary assignment; draws lots for the New World, not China

1681 - Arrives in Mexico on January 27, following a long wait and hard journey

1683-1685 - Missionary work and exploratory expeditions on the California Peninsula

1687 - Arrives in Sonora, Mexico, in March; begins establishing missions and taking the gospel to Pima tribes

1691- Starts exploring and evangelizing in southern Arizona

1695 - Jesuit missionary friend murdered and missions destroyed in March-April uprising; Eusebio arbitrates a peace

1697-1701 - Explores sources of the Río Grande and the San Pedro, Gila, and Colorado Rivers; proves that California is not an island

1711 - Dies at Magdalena mission on March 15, after dedicating a chapel in honor of St. Francis Xavier

1965 - On February 14, a statue of Eusebio Kino is dedicated to represent the State of Arizona in Statuary Hall in the U.S. Capitol in Washington, D.C.

1966 - Archaeologists confirm Padre Kino's burial place on May 21

In the Land I Have Shown You

Lily of the Mohawks

Blessed Kateri Tekakwitha

1656 - 1680

by Ellen Wilson Fielding

In the seventeenth century, French fishermen, fur traders, and explorers were landing in New France, which included not only Quebec but all the lands watered by the St. Lawrence River and the Great Lakes. They traded and made alliances with native tribes such as the Hurons and Algonquins. But for a long time, their small numbers and the vast territories they traveled made it difficult for them to dominate the Indians, as the Spanish in Mexico and South America had done with the more united, sedentary, and agrarian Indians of those regions. By making treaties with the Hurons, the French automatically incurred the bitter opposition of their enemies, the fierce and warlike Iroquois nation—and especially the Mohawks, a branch of the Iroquois.

Childhood in Captivity

This was the inhospitable world into which Kateri (Catherine) Tekakwitha was born in the year 1656, near upstate Auriesville, New York (now the site of the shrine to the North American Jesuit martyrs). Ten years before, about a mile or so away from her village, the great French Jesuit missionary Isaac Jogues had suffered torture and death in the course of the Iroquois' violent rejection of Christianity. Tekakwitha's own family reflected these themes of conquest and strife, since her mother Kahenta was a Canadian Algonquin Christian who had been captured in a Mohawk raid and married to a chief. Isolated from her native people and her religion, Tekakwitha's mother sought solace in her friendship with another Christian captive, Anastasia.

When Tekakwitha was four years old, a smallpox epidemic swept through her village, killing her father, mother, and baby brother, and leaving her face permanently scarred and her eyes and legs weakened. Whenever she left her birch-bark longhouse, she would hold her blanket over her head to shield her eyes from the sun. Her uncle became the new chief, and he and her aunt adopted her into their childless household. There she grew up, eager to work hard to win the love and approval of those around her.

In 1667, when Tekakwitha was eleven, the Mohawks were forced into a grudging peace with the French as a result of a great Iroquois defeat in battle. As part of the peace treaty, Jesuit missionaries were again permitted to visit their villages and explain the Christian teachings to any bold or curious Indians who might want to hear them. For the next eight years, Tekakwitha watched the French

Jesuits from a distance. Her uncle hated Christianity and the Blackrobes who preached it, and through a combination of fear, obedience, and gratitude, Tekakwitha felt unable to seek out the priests against his will. Nevertheless, she deeply desired to learn more about them and about the Christ her mother had known.

The Natural and the Supernatural

God uses the natural as well as the supernatural to accomplish his purposes. The faith of Tekakwitha's dead mother must have fueled her daughter's attraction to Christianity. Perhaps God used her weakness and poor eye sight to begin the process of weaning her away from the world she had grown up in, for they and her scarred face certainly made her feel different from the other girls in her village. She was aware, however, that the effects of the smallpox would not keep away a prospective husband, because her uncle's position as chief would make her a desirable mate. Moreover, she knew how very much her childless aunt and uncle wanted her to marry, not least to ensure their own well-being in old age. It was the men who went out to hunt, and their adopted daughter's husband would not let them go hungry.

This is where the natural and the supernatural aspects of God's approach to Tekakwitha merge most closely. For the young adolescent—who may have heard something about the Virgin Mary but certainly would not have known about nuns or consecrated virgins—refused to marry anyone in these years before she became a Christian. She who had always been meek and eager to please, quick to notice any need her aunt and uncle might have, doing whatever her elders told her, firmly refused them this natural desire which was also the universal fate of any Indian girl.

As a result of Tekakwitha's decision, her aunt and uncle withdrew their approval from her and began treating her like a slave. She suffered, but was not shaken in her resolve to remain a virgin, so unheard of even among Christian Indians. Over time, Tekakwitha's patience and her family's realization that they would not change her mind moderated the severity of her treatment, but their lack of understanding and her uncle's hatred of the Christians remained a constant barrier between them.

A Turning Point

Meanwhile, some of the Mohawks were responding to the Blackrobes' message of love and salvation. About two hundred became Christians before Tekakwitha's baptism, and this drained away strong young lives from the Mohawk settlement, as many of them eventually went north to the Jesuits' Canadian mission. With each departure, the chief saw his tribe's strength dwindling not only in numbers but also in its power to oppose the European onslaught in its many forms. His anger and hatred grew with his frustration and sense of impotence.

Finally, after eight years, a new priest, Father Jacques de Lamberville, arrived to replace Father Boniface, who had died. A day came when an injured foot kept Tekakwitha at home in her lodge while everyone else was out hunting or working in the fields. Father de Lamberville came to visit the now nineteen-year-old, and she found the courage to pour out her longing to become a Christian. Amazed, the priest gently asked the frail girl whether she understood the sacrifices and persecution she would likely face. Then he advised her to pray and to prepare for her baptism by visiting the chapel whenever she could be spared from her work.

A year of learning and prayer went by, ending with a new birth and a new name on Easter Sunday 1676. Tekakwitha received the name of Kateri, for St. Catherine, another virgin saint from a faraway country.

Thriving in Exile

Now Kateri, the half-Algonquin adopted daughter of the chief, felt branded and was treated as an alien. Children threw rocks at her. Her family would not feed her on Sunday, because she would not work on the Lord's day. Her life was threatened. At last, in the fall of 1677, after Kateri had been attacked and almost killed, Father de Lamberville arranged for her to be smuggled out with a Christian from another village who was making the long journey to St. Francis Xavier Mission on the banks of the St. Lawrence, near Montreal. The priest gave her a note to deliver to his fellow Jesuits: "I send you Kateri Tekakwitha. Will you kindly direct her? You will soon discover the treasure I am sending you. Guard it well."

Pursued by Kateri's uncle, the small party managed to elude capture. The long journey they took—covering more than two hundred miles—retraced the path of Kateri's captured mother twenty years earlier. After many days, they reached the mission of St. Francis Xavier safely.

There, Kateri found about 150 Christian families drawn from a number of tribes—Iroquois, Algonquin, Huron—all living the fullness of the Christian life, attending Mass daily, visiting the Blessed Sacrament, and gathering for evening prayer. Many even attended two early-morning Masses before setting out for the fields to work. "The whole village could be taken for a monastery," a visiting bishop once wrote, and Kateri thrived spiritually in this atmosphere. She carved crosses on the bark of the trees marking her daily route to the spring for water. She drank in all she could learn of Christianity from Anastasia, once her mother's friend— and she traveled the route to Christian perfection by leaps and bounds in these last few years of her life.

Seeking Union with Christ

After her First Communion on Christmas Day 1677, Kateri's desire to demonstrate her love for God grew even greater. Everything she did was offered to God as prayer. She filled every moment of the day with work, making and embroidering clothes and preparing birch bark for canoes and furniture. She spent hours every night in prayer, and often absented herself from the common main meal of the day to fast. She once said that she offered her soul to Christ the Lord in the Blessed Sacrament, and her body to Christ the Lord hanging on the cross.

Kateri also endured a time of suffering at the mission when one woman there falsely accused her of drawing her husband into adultery. Over time, her patient virtue and kindness—even to those who accused and shunned her—won them over.

When those close to her tried to convince Kateri to marry, she resolutely told them that she belonged only to Jesus. Father Pierre Cholenec, her spiritual director at the mission, recognized this as a true vocation and allowed her to make her long-held vow of chastity publicly in the church at Mass in 1679. After her consecration, Kateri exchanged her red blanket for a blue one in honor of Mary, and wore the braids of a young unmarried Iroquois girl.

Never strong, Kateri grew progressively weaker. She suffered from severe headaches, stomachaches, and fever. But her love for God burned so strongly that the other women at the mission would try to sit near her in church. They said that looking at her was the best preparation for Communion.

Kateri's strength drained fast throughout her final Lent in 1680. Near the end, she foretold the day and time of her own death, which occurred on April 17, Wednesday of Holy Week. Her last words were "Jesus, Mary, I love you." She was twenty-four years old. As Kateri's soul parted from her body, Father Cholenec and the other onlookers watched her face change. The scarring from smallpox and the drawn look of her illnesses gave way to a radiant beauty. At the amazed outcry, the other Frenchmen at the mission hurried to see her body, and were so impressed that they built her coffin leaving Kateri's face open to view.

Almost immediately, the few small articles she owned—her food bowl, ragged clothing, crucifix, even the dust from her gravesite—became relics to the Indians, and miracles began to be reported. Kateri Tekakwitha was beatified by Pope John Paul II on June 22, 1980, three hundred years after her death. Today, the frail young woman with the downcast eyes and the blanket draped protectively over her head is honored with a statue in the National Shrine of the Immaculate Conception in Washington, D.C. The feast day of this Native American holy woman shared by Canadians and Americans is celebrated on July 14.

Lily of the Mohawks

This popular prayer expresses many of Kateri Tekakwitha's saintly qualities.

Litany of Blessed Kateri Tekakwitha

Lord, have mercy on us.
Christ, have mercy on us.
Lord, have mercy on us.
Christ, hear us.
Christ, graciously hear us.
God the Father of Heaven, have mercy on us.
God the Son, Redeemer of the World, have mercy on us.
God the Holy Ghost, have mercy on us.
Holy Trinity, one God, have mercy on us.

Kateri, lily of purity, pray for us.
Kateri, consoler of the heart of Jesus, pray for us.
Kateri, bright light for all Indians, pray for us.
Kateri, courage of the afflicted, pray for us.
Kateri, lover of the cross of Jesus, pray for us.
Kateri, flower of fortitude for the persecuted, pray for us.
Kateri, unshakable in temptations, pray for us.
Kateri, full of patience in suffering, pray for us.
Kateri, keeper of your virginity in persecutions, pray for us.

Kateri, leader of many Indians to the true faith through your love for Mary, pray for us.

Kateri, who loved Jesus in the Blessed Sacrament, pray for us.

Kateri, lover of penance, pray for us.

Kateri, who traveled many miles to learn the faith, pray for us.

Kateri, steadfast in all prayer, pray for us.

Kateri, who loved to pray the rosary for all people, pray for us.

Kateri, example to your people in all virtues, pray for us.

Kateri, humble servant to the sick, pray for us.

Kateri, who by your love of humility, gave joy to the angels, pray for us.

Kateri, your holy death gave strength to all Indians to love Jesus and Mary, pray for us.

Kateri, whose scarred face in life became beautiful after death, pray for us.

Lamb of God, who takes away the sins of the world, spare us, O Lord.

Lamb of God, who takes away the sins of the world, graciously hear us, O Lord.

Lamb of God, who takes away the sins of the world, have mercy on us.

Let us pray.

O Jesus, who gave Kateri to the Indians as an example of purity, teach all men to love purity, and to console your immaculate Mother Mary through the lily, Kateri Tekakwitha, and your Holy Cross. Amen.

Kateri Tekakwitha, pray for us.

The Life of Kateri Tekakwitha

1656 - Born in the village of Ossernenon, the daughter of a Mohawk chief (in some accounts given the name Kenhoronkwa) and an Algonquin Christian, Kahenta

1660 - Adopted into her uncle's household after her parents die in a smallpox epidemic; the tribe moves to a new village, Gandawague

1667 - Jesuit missionaries briefly visit Tekakwitha's village as part of the terms of a peace treaty with the French after the Iroquois are defeated in battle and later settle there, converting many of the villagers

1675 - Father Jacques de Lamberville visits Tekakwitha's longhouse, and she tells him of her desire to become a Christian

1676 - Baptized on Easter Sunday, April 5, and receives the name Kateri in honor of St. Catherine

1677 - Escapes to St. Francis Xavier Mission near Montreal; receives her First Communion on Christmas Day

1679 - Makes a public vow of chastity, perpetually consecrating her virginity to Christ, on March 25, the feast of the Annunciation

1680 - Dies on April 17, at the age of tenty-four

1980 - Beatified by Pope John Paul II on June 22

The Widow of Montreal

Saint Marguerite d'Youville

1701 - 1771

by Jeanne Kun

May 18, 1765—Mother Marguerite d'Youville and her sisters watched with heavy hearts, smoke burning their tear-filled eyes, as flames raged through the General Hospital of Montreal. The building had been their home as well as home to scores of the city's sick and infirm whom they nursed there. Then Marguerite gathered her courage—as she had done so many times throughout her life—and said, "Let us kneel and say the *Te Deum* to thank God for the cross he has seen fit to send us." Forty hours later, after the fire was finally put out, 182 buildings—one-quarter of the city of Montreal—had been destroyed.

This was not the first time Marguerite d'Youville had known such loss. Twenty years earlier, her house, where she had also sheltered the elderly and ailing, was gutted by fire. Nor was she a stranger to other hardships. Her marriage had been difficult, and four of her children died in infancy.

Widowed at the age of twenty-nine when her profligate husband died, she was left with the burden of his many debts and shameful reputation. Yet the more God had taken from Marguerite, the more she had generously given to him.

The Early Years

Born on October 15, 1701, in Varennes, near Montreal, Marguerite was the eldest of the six children of Christophe Dufrost de Lajemmerais and his wife, Marie Renée. Marguerite's father died when she was seven years old. When she was eleven, she was sent to the Ursuline school in Quebec to prepare for her First Communion and to learn skills to help her mother take care of the home and family.

Ten years later, Marguerite married a charming suitor, François d'Youville, unaware that he was an unscrupulous spendthrift. It wasn't long before he showed himself to be a selfish man with little regard for his wife. He frequently spent long periods of time away from home, and Marguerite came to realize that he made his income secretly selling liquor to the Indians around Montreal—a practice banned by the French colony's government. Nonetheless, Marguerite cared for François when he became ill as a result of his dissolute lifestyle and grieved at his death. Now left to raise two young sons on her own, Marguerite opened a small shop and slowly paid off her husband's debts.

Rather than becoming embittered by all these difficulties, Madame d'Youville saw them as opportunities to draw closer to God. She attended Mass daily, joined the Confraternity of the Holy Family, and grew in love for God through prayer. Her devotion to "the Eternal Father" and her trust in his loving providence became the keynote of her life. It was also during these early years of her widow-hood that she began to visit the poor and sick throughout the city.

Marguerite's spiritual director, Father Louis Normant, saw how compassionately she reached out to the destitute. He realized that her own experiences of suffering had given her valuable spiritual and practical training and encouraged her charitable work. He also noted her talent for managing her shop efficiently and eliminating François' debts, and fore-saw great works for her in the future.

Dedication to the Poor

In November 1737, Marguerite, with her son Charles, converted her house into a home for the poor and aged. On December 31, she and three like-minded companions privately consecrated themselves to the service of the poor. The following year Marguerite moved to a larger house so she could accommodate more needy people, and her associates moved in with her. Now living together under the same roof, the four women renewed their conse-cration under Father Normant's guidance.

In the eighteenth century, new religious communities could not be formed in France or its colonies without the approval of the king—something which was usually diffi-cult to gain because religious orders were supported by subsidies taken from the royal purse. Thus, for the next fif-teen years, Madame d'Youville and her companions actively carried out their works of mercy as a "free association of pious women." However, they were neither civilly nor canonically recognized as a religious congregation.

At the time Marguerite invited her coworkers to move in with her, she was still criticized as the widow of the disreputable d'Youville. Many Montrealers considered her charitable activities a front for continuing her husband's illegal bootlegging business. Marguerite and her companions were even pelted with stones in the street and publicly refused Communion, and called *les soeurs grises*, or "the tipsy sisters."

When the sisters' first house burned early in 1745, they had to find new lodgings for themselves and the people they cared for. They also saw this tragedy as an opportunity to deepen their commitment as a sisterhood by sharing all their possessions in common. At their request, Father Normant wrote a provisional rule of life for them— the foundation stone of the future congregation—which they signed on February 2.

A Firm Foundation

Slowly, as they saw the sisters' true worth, many of the townspeople changed their opinions of Marguerite and her sisters. After the fire, many came to their assistance. By 1747, circumstances were ripe for the sisters to be given charge of Montreal's General Hospital, the work Father Normant had long envisioned for Marguerite. The religious brothers who founded the hospital in 1694 and had staffed it for many years could no longer carry on this responsibility, and the building was in dire need of repairs. Its restoration and management was entrusted to Madame d'Youville, with the provision that she and her sisters also assume the hospital's enormous debt of 49,000 livres. Undaunted, Marguerite put her confidence in the Eternal Father.

The sisters took in the sick, the disabled, the aged, the mentally unbalanced, and the incurable of either sex. They turned no one away. The General Hospital not only served the afflicted, it also became the cradle of a new religious institute. Young women impressed by the sisters' witness asked Madame d'Youville to accept them as novices. Finally, in 1753, King Louis XV of France granted the sisters royal sanction as a religious congregation. Two years later, the bishop of Quebec formally approved their rule, recognizing them as the "Sisters of Charity of Montreal." The French word for "tipsy" also means "grey," so with a sense of humor and as a sign of humility, the sisters chose to wear grey-colored habits. Thus, the former "tipsy sisters" also became known as the "Grey Nuns"—but it was now with respect and admiration that their fellow Montrealers called them *les Soeurs Grises.*

The Eternal Father Provides

These years of struggle and growth for the Grey Nuns were also marked by economic hardship and political upheaval in Canada. The war that had flared up on the Continent between France and England reached the colonies in the New World, too. As the British battled the French Canadians and their Indian allies, the wards of the General Hospital were filled with the wounded of both sides.

Mother d'Youville even ransomed English captives from Indians who intended to torture them to death. On one occasion, an English soldier by the name of Southworth rushed into the hospital, pursued by a brave brandishing a tomahawk. Mother d'Youville calmly hid the soldier under the large canvas tent she and another sister were sewing. Later, during the siege of Montreal, cannons were aimed to fire on the large stone hospital, fortress-like in appearance. It was Southworth who stopped the bombardment just in the nick of time, rushing to his commander to explain the work of the sisters who had saved his life there.

Quebec fell to the British in 1759 with General Wolfe's victory over General Montcalm, and Montreal surrendered in 1760. By the provisions of the Treaty of Paris, all of Canada came under the British flag in 1763. Because of damages and the exorbitant cost of food and other necessities during the war, the General Hospital was again heavily in debt. Nevertheless, Mother d'Youville bought and ran farms to ease their needs and support her large "family" of 118 patients, sisters, and boarders.

Rather than cutting back during these lean years, the Grey Nuns expanded their charitable efforts. In addition to continuing their care for the sick, they offered closed retreats for women, supported needy seminarians, and took in abandoned babies.

Once, after checking her accounts, Mother d'Youville discovered that she had only one small silver coin left. At that moment, a poor woman came to claim her payment for nursing a baby in their care—a payment of the exact amount of the coin. Marguerite reached into her pocket, only to find a whole handful of coins! Amazed, she reached into her other pocket and brought out yet another handful! At another time, when the sisters and their patients were close to starving, six barrels of flour inexplicably "appeared" in their dining room. The Eternal Father never failed to care for his daughters and for the poor they served.

A Mission Fulfilled

When Montreal was devastated by the great fire of 1765, Indians whom Marguerite and her sisters had nursed during a smallpox epidemic sold many of their treasured possessions and gave the money toward rebuilding the hospital. Public collections were also taken up by the people of London to relieve the suffering Montrealers, who were now under British rule. "To adore the designs of God and to submit to his will—that is what we have all tried our best to do!" Marguerite wrote as she took up the enormous work of building a new hospital.

During the last years of her life, Mother d'Youville delighted in the harmony and affection she saw in the growing congregation that surrounded her: "All the riches in the world cannot equal the happiness of living together in unity," she wrote. A warm and loving mother, she was gratified to see that she had taught the sisters well.

At Marguerite's death in 1771, one of her first companions remarked, "When we write her epitaph, we must remember first our Mother's mission of love. We must entrust her secret to those who will follow us, and tell them that, yes, she loved greatly. . . She loved greatly, Jesus Christ and the poor!"

Mother Marguerite d'Youville was canonized by Pope John Paul II in 1990, the first native-born Canadian to be declared a saint. Today Marguerite's spiritual daughters continue her mission serving the poor and sick throughout Canada, the United States, Japan, Africa, and South America.

The Widow of Montreal

The Grey Nuns of the Sacred Heart were established in 1921 to continue the mission of Marguerite d'Youville in the United States. Their spirituality, which is based on four central metaphors rooted in the seventeenth-century school of French spirituality, reflects the original inspiration and energy of Montreal's Grey Nuns.

Sacred Heart

"Learn from the heart of the Father, the attitudes of love, tender concern, and compassion. . ."

—Marguerite d'Youville

The focus is on the interior life. It is a symbol and an invitation to communion with God. In the biblical sense, the heart is a symbol of all that is part of being a human person—mind, thought, emotions, love . . . everything.

Divine Providence

"I leave all to Divine Providence. All will happen that is pleasing to God."

—Marguerite d'Youville

This metaphor speaks of bold action, undertaken with appropriate fear and trepidation, but with the faith that all of our needs will be met. It has a noble and proud history both in our congregation and in the greater Christian tradition.

Cross

"I could hardly make myself believe that God would not save this house which was the refuge of the poor."

—Marguerite d'Youville

Loss, pain, and diminishment can lead to new hope and new life. That is what is contained in this symbol. It is the Cross of Christ that allows us to find a source of joy and to look upon pain and loss as signs of God's love.

Eternal Father

"Eternal Father, you are the source of all good."

—Marguerite d'Youville

It is important to understand the critical and privileged place for healing and liberation that this metaphor has provided, both in the early Christian community and in the life of Marguerite as well.

The Life of Marguerite d'Youville

1701 - Born on October 15 at Varennes, near Montreal, the oldest child of Christophe Dufrost de Lajemmerais and his wife, Marie Renée

1722 - Marries François d'Youville on August 12

1730 - Widowed at the age of twenty-nine; only two of her six children survive beyond infancy

1737 - Opens her home to the infirm; Marguerite and three companions privately consecrate themselves to serving the poor

1745 - Marguerite and her associates sign a provisional rule of life written at their request by Father Louis Normant

1747 - Becomes directress of Montreal's General Hospital

1753 - The sisters receive royal sanction from King Louis XV of France as a religious congregation

1755 - On June 15, Bishop de Pontbriand of Quebec approves the sisters' rule, and they adopt grey habits

1765 - The General Hospital of Montreal is destroyed by fire on May 18

1771 - Dies on December 23

1959 - Beatified on May 3 by Pope John XXIII, who calls Marguerite the "Mother of Universal Charity"

1990 - Canonized by Pope John Paul II on December 9; her feast day is October 16

In the Land I Have Shown You

Turning Loss into Triumph

Saint Elizabeth Ann Seton

1774 - 1821

by Ellen Wilson Fielding

We may think of the late eighteenth and early nineteenth centuries as a time of formal, stilted language and carefully contained emotions. When we read historic documents from that time, we come across long sentences filled with high-flown and daunting language.

Yet across that gulf of two centuries comes the warm, open voice of Elizabeth Ann Bayley Seton:

> A day of days for me, Amabilia. I have been where?—to the Church of St. Peter with the cross on top instead of a weathercock! That is mischievous—but I mean I have been to what is called here among so many churches the Catholic Church. When I turned the corner of the street it is in— "Here, my God, I go," I said, "heart all to You."

As soon as we hear her speak, we know that we have found someone ideally suited to be our friend, just as so many of her contemporaries found her.

Early Sorrow and Loss

Elizabeth Ann Bayley was born in New York City on August 28, 1774, as the First Continental Congress was preparing to meet in Philadelphia. Both her grandmothers were French Huguenots—Protestants who fled to America because of persecution. Her maternal grandfather was an Episcopalian minister. Her father, a doctor energetically devoted to the poor, had imbibed the Enlightenment-era lack of interest in religious matters. Elizabeth belonged to a well-off, well-connected family. Yet early in her life a note of sorrow and loss was introduced, which would be repeated throughout her forty-six years of life.

Her mother died when Elizabeth was almost three. Dr. Bayley soon married a young bride to care for the three Bayley girls—Mary, Elizabeth, and baby Kitty—though the stepmother was always cool toward her husband's children. Little Kitty died soon after the new Mrs. Bayley's arrival, and these early deaths set Elizabeth's thoughts on heaven. Years later, in notes labeled *Dear Remembrances*, she recalls someone asking why she was not crying for her dead sister. "I'm not crying because Kitty has gone to heaven. And I wish I could go to heaven to be with my mother, too!"

The new Mrs. Bayley increasingly concentrated on her own growing family while Elizabeth's beloved but distant father worked long hours. She studied hard to please him, devoting herself especially to learning French and music, which he loved. When Elizabeth was fourteen, her father sailed to England for a lengthy stay, so the two sisters were sent to visit their uncle in rural New Rochelle. A year went by without so much as a letter from Dr. Bayley.

Left with much time to think, Elizabeth grew increasingly devoted to her heavenly Father, poring over her Bible and learning by heart the psalms and much of the New Testament. She also explored the beautiful New Rochelle countryside. Years later she recalled one day's outing in particular, when she:

> Set off in the woods, soon found an outlet in a meadow; and a chestnut tree with several young ones growing around it, found rich moss under it and a warm sun. Here, then, was a sweet bed— the air still, a clear blue vault above—the numberless sounds of spring melody and joy—the sweet clovers and wildflowers I had got by the way, and a heart as innocent as human heart could be, filled with enthusiastic love to God and admiration of his works.

Starting a New Family

When Elizabeth was almost sixteen, her father returned from England, and she went back to what she hoped to be a joyful reunion in New York. But relations between husband and wife, and between stepmother and stepdaughter, had not improved. Some sort of family crisis or explosion occurred, which Elizabeth recorded in these bewildered, wounded words: "Family disagreement. Could not guess why when I spoke kindly to relations, they did not speak to me."

Elizabeth alternately lived with her maternal aunt and her now-married older sister. She and her father grew closer, and she entered the New York social life of families like the Barclays, Roosevelts, Van Cortlandts, and Jays. At eighteen, she met and soon married William Magee Seton and set up her own dearly cherished household, including children she could hug to her affectionate heart.

Elizabeth's time of good fortune did not close her heart to the troubles of Dr. Bayley's beloved poor. She founded a society—dubbed by some the "Protestant Sisters of Charity"— to raise money for the poor, visit them, and care for their sick. Her husband's large family loved and admired Elizabeth and looked to her as an example.

A Long Journey

Elizabeth's long route to the Catholic Church began with William's declining fortunes. After his father died in 1798, William struggled to care for seven younger brothers and sisters, while hostilities between France and England played havoc with his shipping business. Elizabeth spent hours after the children were in bed helping him with his accounts and business correspondence, but in 1801, William was forced to declare bankruptcy. At the same time, Elizabeth's father caught yellow fever from a shipload of Irish immigrants he had hurried to care for.

Elizabeth was frantic not only with anxiety about her father's health, but with concern for his soul. In her desperation, she offered God her infant daughter's life for her father's salvation: God granted the request, though without accepting the sacrifice. (Kitty would instead be by far the longest-lived of all Elizabeth's children, reaching the age of ninety-one.)

William had also paid little attention to religious matters, but his declining health, as well as Elizabeth's heartfelt prayers and sacrifices, began to win him over. Gravely ill with tuberculosis, William decided to visit his longtime business friends, the Filicchis, in the warmer climate of Italy. Late in 1803, Elizabeth, William, and eight-year-old Anna Maria set sail for Livorno, Italy.

Everything went wrong. The ship was refused permission to dock because of fears that an epidemic in New York might be passed on by the passengers. The Setons were given damp, cold, jail-like housing during the monthlong quarantine. William deteriorated rapidly, while Elizabeth tried both to cheer him and to prepare him for death. She also had to calm and amuse little Anna Maria, skipping rope with her to keep warm in their chilly lodgings. She kept her fears and loneliness for the journal-letter she was writing to her favorite sister-in-law, Rebecca.

"How Happy We Would Be"

William survived quarantine long enough to spend a few days in the Filicchis' welcoming home. Then, at the age of twenty-nine, Elizabeth found herself an impoverished widow with five young children. During the long wait for a return ship to America, the Filicchis took Elizabeth into their hearts. They were devout Catholics, and Elizabeth's stay gave her time to respond to the appeal of Catholicism.

On her walks, she was drawn to the Catholic churches with their red vigil lamps attesting to the presence of Christ in the Eucharist. She, who had seen so many loved ones pass beyond the reach of her touch, began to hunger for the Eucharist that would put Christ in physical reach of her. She wrote to Rebecca: "How happy would we be if we believed what these dear souls believe! In their faith they possess God in the Sacrament; they find him in their churches; they see him come to them when they are sick."

After an eight-month absence, Elizabeth returned home and was reunited with her younger children. She was worried and distracted not only by financial problems, but by her increasing certainty that God was calling her into the Catholic Church. Anti-Catholic feeling was strong in early America, and ugly incidents made it clear to Elizabeth how she was jeopardizing her family's future. Rebecca, her soul mate, sympathized, but she too was dying of tuberculosis, and could only murmur: "Thy people shall be my people, and thy God, my God" (Ruth 1:16). On March 14, 1805, Elizabeth was received into the Catholic Church. She was thirty years old.

The next few years were difficult for Elizabeth. As she had foreseen, a number of friends and relations abandoned her when she entered the Church. The pupils she was struggling to teach melted away because their Protestant parents would not entrust them to Catholic teaching. Then Elizabeth was asked by Father William Du Bourg, the president of St. Mary's Seminary in Baltimore, to establish a school for girls.

The Sisters of Charity

Elizabeth and her children left New York for Baltimore where, in the summer of 1808, she opened the first parochial school in the United States. Soon several young women who were interested in becoming nuns joined her. Elizabeth had been attracted to the religious life since her conversion, but had her responsibility toward her children to consider. Now, under the guidance of Archbishop John Carroll, the first bishop of the United States, Elizabeth and her companions established an American religious order, adopting as their rule that of St. Vincent de Paul's Daughters of Charity.

One highly unusual condition set by Elizabeth when she formed the order was that she be allowed to bring up her children, ranging in age from six to thirteen. (Her daughters remained with her, while her sons attended boarding school nearby.) The habit she chose was also unusual: her black widow's clothes, complete with short cape and bonnet. Four years after becoming a Catholic, she pronounced her vows and was appointed head of her little community. Thus, Mrs. Seton became Mother Seton.

In 1809, property near Emmitsburg in northwestern Maryland was purchased where a larger school building and residence for the sisters were built with funds contributed by a friend. Elizabeth, her daughters, and the members of her new order moved into the "Stone House," where the roof leaked and water had to be carried from a distant spring. Winter was hard in this mountainous, rural region and there was much sickness. The order's first spiritual adviser caused great difficulties. By the first spring, Elizabeth's sisters-in-law Harriet and Cecilia, who had joined her, died. Elizabeth maintained her resolve, mothering her community with affection, firmness, and indomitable trust in God.

In the next few years the order grew and the school thrived, but Elizabeth's personal sufferings did not lessen. Her two sons caused her sleepless nights because of their lukewarmness and many false starts in life. Her firstborn, sixteen-year-old Anna Maria, died a painful death that left Elizabeth resigned to God's will, but emotionally devastated. Not long after, Anna Maria's sister Rebecca joined the growing row of gravestones in the community cemetery.

Meanwhile, Elizabeth became mother to a growing community of nuns and the schoolchildren they taught. She wrote warm, humorous, but wise letters to many of the girls after they left school, and to some of the nearby seminarians as well. She saw her order begin to spread before she died, though she could never have imagined its future spectacular growth. (By the mid-1970s, the Sisters of Charity numbered over eight thousand nuns, with sixty-seven hospitals and more than six hundred elementary and high schools.)

". . . And Then Eternity"

She who had seen so many sickbeds and deathbeds proved a model patient during her long decline into the family disease, tuberculosis. Elizabeth's life had been a training ground in trusting obedience to the Father's will, and she was more than ready to surrender her life to God. As one of the nuns tried to administer her medicine early in January 1821, she brushed it aside, murmuring, "One more Communion and then Eternity." Elizabeth Ann Bayley Seton died early on the morning of January 4, 1821. In 1975, she was canonized as the first native-born American saint.

Turning Loss into Triumph

When the Setons arrived in Italy in 1803, they were quarantined in a lazaretto because it was feared that the ship on which they had sailed carried yellow fever from New York. William, already gravely ill with tuberculosis, rapidly declined, and shortly after being released from quarantine, died. The following account is from a journal written by Elizabeth for her sister-in-law.

19th November 1803—10 o'clock at night.

". . . Now, on the ship-mattresses spread on this cool floor, my William and Anna [oldest daughter] are sound asleep; and I trust that God, who has given him strength to go through a day of such exertion, will carry us on. He is our all indeed. My eyes smart so much with crying, wind and fatigue, that I must close them and lift up my heart.

Sleep won't come very easily. If you had seen little Anna's arms clasped round my neck at her prayers, while the tears rolled a stream, how you would love her! I read her to sleep, little pieces of trust in God. She said,

"Mamma, if papa should die here—"

"But God will be with us."

God is with us, and if sufferings abound in us, his consolations also greatly abound, and far exceed all utterance. If the wind (for it is said there were never such storms at this season) that now almost puts our my lamp and blows on my William through every crevice, and over our chimney like loud thunder, could come from any but his command, or if the circumstances that have placed us in so forlorn a situation were not guided by his hand—miserable indeed would be our case. Within this hour he has had a violent fit of coughing so as to bring up blood, which agitates and distresses him through all his endeavors to hide it. What shall we say? This is the hour of trial. The Lord supports and strengthens us in it. . . .

Monday [26th December]

[William] was so impatient to be gone that I could scarcely persuade him to wet his lips, but continued calling his Redeemer to pardon and release him. As he always would have his door shut, I had no interruption. Carleton [Elizabeth's half-brother] kept Anna out of the way; and every promise in the Scriptures and prayer I could remember I continually repeated to him, which seemed to be his only relief. When I stopped to give him anything:

"Why do you do it? What do I want? I want to be in heaven. Pray. Pray for my soul."

He said he felt so comfortable an assurance that his Redeemer would receive him that he saw his dear little Tat [youngest daughter, Rebecca] smiling before him; and told Anna:

"Oh, if your father could take you with him!"

At four, the hard struggle ceased. Nature sank into a settled sob:

"My dear wife—and little ones"—"My Christ Jesus, have mercy and receive me," was all I could distinguish; and again, repeated, "My Christ Jesus," until a quarter past seven, when the dear soul took its flight to the Blessed Exchange it so much longed for.

I often asked him, when he could not speak,

"You feel, my love, that you are going to your Redeemer?" and he motioned "yes" with a look of peace.

At a quarter past seven on Tuesday morning, 27th December, his soul was released—and mine from a struggle next to death. ⟨⟩

The Life of Elizabeth Ann Seton

1774 - Born on August 28 in New York City, the second daughter of Dr. Richard Bayley and his first wife, Catherine Charlton

1777 - Elizabeth's mother dies

1794 - Marries William Magee Seton on January 25; the couple have five children within the next eight years

1803 - Elizabeth and William arrive in Italy on November 18; William dies of tuberculosis on December 26

1805 - Elizabeth is received into the Catholic Church March 14, and makes her First Communion on the feast of the Annunciation, March 25

1808 - Opens a girls' school in Baltimore—the first parochial school in America—and takes the first steps toward forming a religious community, the Sisters of Charity

1809 - Pronounces her first vows in the presence of Archbishop John Carroll on March 25; Elizabeth and four companions receive their habits on June 1 and soon move into the Stone House in Emmitsburg, Maryland; her sons, William and Richard, attend boys' academies under the direction of the Sulpician Fathers while her daughters, Anna Maria, Catherine, and Rebecca, remain with her

1812 - Elizabeth's sixteen-year-old daughter Anna Maria, a postulant in the community, dies on March 12

1816 - Elizabeth's fourteen-year-old daughter Rebecca dies

1821 - Mother Elizabeth Ann Seton dies on January 4 in Emmitsburg with her community of sisters around her

1963 - Beatified by Pope John XXIII on March 17

1975 - Canonized by Pope Paul VI on September 14; her feast day is January 4

Photo: Columbia University Archives—Columbiana Library.

Freedom in Christ

Venerable Pierre Toussaint
1766 - 1853

by Ellen Wilson Fielding

Venerable Pierre Toussaint lived an unusual life for an American colonist. He was a slave, but he supported the family who owned him. He was a hairdresser who counseled his customers and became so wealthy that he was the benefactor of many in New York City. As a black Catholic, he was a member of two minority groups, but he did not allow prejudice to embitter him. Nearly two hundred years after his death, Toussaint's quiet life and holiness led Church officials to introduce his cause for canonization.

Toussaint was born into a Haitian slave family in 1766. He was just turning ten when the colonists in America signed a document stating that "all men are created equal," but slavery would persist in the United States throughout Pierre Toussaint's long lifetime. In Haiti, however, matters unfolded differently.

Pierre was bright and quick and soon caught the attention of his well-disposed French slave master, Jean Bérard. Bérard taught the boy to read and write and gave him the run of the plantation library. Like their master and mistress, the Toussaints were baptized and reared as devout Catholics. Pierre was a house slave rather than a field slave, and came to identify himself with the pressing concerns of the Bérard family.

Refuge in New York

When the elder Bérards decided to resettle in France, they entrusted the running of the plantation to their oldest son, Jean Jacques, who retained Pierre, by now a young adult, with him. However, the family's affairs began taking a turn for the worse when unrest among Haiti's slave population surfaced. Rumors of a large-scale slave insurrection worried the island's plantation owners. In 1787, Jean Jacques and his wife, Marie Elizabeth, relocated to New York City, hoping to return to Haiti when the situation quieted down. They took with them Madame Bérard's sisters as well as Pierre, his beloved younger sister Rosalie, his aunt, and a few other slaves.

Once settled in New York, the Bérards arranged for Pierre to be apprenticed to a hairdresser to learn the trade. A talented hairdresser with excellent social skills could prosper greatly if he caught the attention of the upper echelons of society. Pierre soon found his services in great demand among the city's elite, who included the wife of Alexander Hamilton and the daughters of Revolutionary War General Philip Schuyler.

A Hairdresser and Confidant

Pierre's clients appreciated not only his skill but his social tact as well. One woman noted, "Some of the most pleasant hours I pass are in conversation with Toussaint while he is dressing my hair." The women confided their most private concerns and troubles to him, confident that he would not betray them to anyone else. When anyone sought to pry other women's stories from him, he would simply reply, "Toussaint dresses hair; he is no news journal."

Such discretion is common to many a pleasant, socially adept hairdresser today. What made Pierre different was his deep love and faith in God, which moved him to advise his customers to confide their cares and troubles to Christ. He counseled them to make all their decisions in the light of their faith. Women agonized over difficult or unfaithful spouses, wayward children, ailing family and friends, and financial crises. When they unpacked their troubles for Pierre's inspection, the hairdresser gave them the same advice he followed himself: untiring prayer and patient trust in God. As a result, many seeming social butterflies found their way onto Pierre's personal prayer list.

Unlike many French men of the time—whose religious practice was slack at best—Pierre was devoted to Jesus and to the Church. New York had not yet experienced the great waves of Catholic immigration that would transform the city by the middle of the 1800s, and Catholics were still a very conspicuous and distrusted minority—as though Pierre needed to belong to another conspicuous minority!

Still, Toussaint began each day with the 6:00 Mass at St. Peter's Church (where a fellow communicant would soon be the Protestant convert, Elizabeth Ann Seton). Then he would return home to do his household work for the Bérards before setting out for his appointments with clients. Although his circumstances were unusual—the slave of French Catholics living in Anglo-Protestant New York City—Pierre did not act embarrassed, embattled, or defensive about his unusual position. Instead, those he met were struck by his faith-filled serenity.

The Path to Freedom and Family

Life became even more anomalous after Jean Jacques Bérard returned alone to Haiti in an effort to salvage his plantation following the slave revolts. Not only had the insurrections left him nothing to recoup, but Monsieur Bérard soon died. His wife, anxiously awaiting his return in New York, sank into deep depression at the double loss of her husband and any means of financial support. From that point on, Pierre became the breadwinner of this oddly constituted family.

Pierre was by now earning enough not only to support Madame Bérard, but to maintain the upper-class lifestyle that seemed so necessary to her happiness. He managed her finances and even undertook to arrange parties and social events to help bring her out of her despondency. Realizing that the distressed widow would not feel comfortable allowing him to support her and organize her life for her if he were a free man, Pierre even declined Madame Bérard's offer to free him after her husband's death.

After some years of widowhood, Madame Bérard remarried. She died in 1807, thanking Pierre over and over again for all he had done for her, and finally bestowing on him his long-awaited freedom. Pierre was by this time over forty years old and still unmarried. He had long loved a young Haitian woman named Juliette Noel, but the two had postponed their wedding until his responsibilities for Madame Bérard and her household were fulfilled and he could attain the status of a free man. That time had finally arrived.

The Toussaints' delayed marriage was a happy one. Juliette was warmhearted and outgoing, and the couple were united in their desire to help those around them who were less fortunate. Over the years, Pierre and Juliette opened their home to many orphans and destitute people. One cloud in their life together was that they could not have children of their own. However, they lovingly adopted their niece Euphemia, the orphaned daughter of Rosalie, whose freedom Pierre had earlier purchased.

A Generous Heart

Over the years, Pierre's charitable gifts accumulated. He had a particular tenderness for slaves and black orphans. He purchased freedom for many of the slaves, and sheltered some of the orphans in his own home. In his efforts to care for the poor, this black man and former slave found himself collaborating with America's first native-born citizen saint, Elizabeth Ann Seton. Pierre assisted the Sisters of Charity, founded by Mother Seton, in establishing one of the first orphanages in New York. Pierre also figured as a major contributor and fund-raiser for the city's first cathedral, old St. Patrick's in lower Manhattan. He gave generously to a Catholic school for blacks established on Canal Street, and also assisted a religious order for black women in Baltimore.

However, Pierre did more than just dole out money. During one of the periodic yellow fever epidemics that terrorized congested cities in that era, he risked his own life by remaining in the city to care for the sick and dying. Someone asked him what consoling words he had found for a woman who had just lost a beloved family member. "I could only take her hand," he replied, "and weep with her, and then I went away; there was nothing to be said."

Kindness in the Face of Prejudice

The Bérards had been kind and generous people who valued Pierre's gifts and person. But Toussaint lived with routine racial discrimination throughout his life. Though a major force behind the building of St. Patrick's, he and his wife were once turned away from the church by an usher who did not know who he was. A horrified trustee attempted to put things right by an apology, but that couldn't assure Pierre of a future welcome there under similar circumstances. Throughout his life, the busy hairdresser had to make his way on foot to all of his appointments, because carriage drivers did not convey black people.

Like others of his skin color, then and later, Pierre experienced casual slights, humiliations, and daily insults. Somehow he kept himself free from both resentment and any form of submission. After years of slavery, he chose not to enslave his emotions to the behavior of other people. He knew that nothing could rob him of his human dignity, which belonged to him as a child of God. Jesus had, after all, chosen to die for him. In response to this unmatchable gift, Toussaint strove to give himself to God in turn, saying, "Jesus can give you nothing so precious as himself, as his own mind. Do not think that any faith in him can do you good if you do not try to be pure and true like him."

Pierre Toussaint survived into an active old age. On June 30, 1853, two years after the death of his beloved Juliette, he died at the age of eighty-seven. Great crowds who had benefited from his financial generosity, personal charity, and counsel thronged the funeral Mass. The New York newspapers published obituaries testifying to his services to the city's needy. But perhaps the best testimonial to Pierre was that once given by General Schuyler: "I have known Christians who were not gentlemen or gentlemen who were not Christians— but one man I know who is both—and that man is Black."

The Transforming Light of Faith

In 1968, New York's Terence Cardinal Cooke introduced Pierre Toussaint's cause for canonization. His successor, John Cardinal O'Connor, who enthusiastically backed Toussaint's cause, moved his remains from their resting place in old St. Patrick's cemetery to the crypt below the main altar of the current St. Patrick's Cathedral. He is the only layman interred in the burial place of bishops and cardinals.

During his 1995 visit to St. Patrick's, Pope John Paul II spoke movingly of Toussaint:

> What is so extraordinary about this man? He radiated a most serene and joyful faith, nourished daily by the Eucharist and visits to the Blessed Sacrament. In the face of constant,

painful discrimination he understood, as few have understood, the meaning of the words, "Father, forgive them; they do not know what they are doing." No treasure is as uplifting and transforming as the light of faith.

Toussaint received from Pope John Paul II the title "Venerable" in 1996.

Pierre Toussaint didn't start an order, like Francis of Assisi. He wasn't known as a miracle worker, like Anthony of Padua. He wasn't a mystic like Catherine of Siena or a great theologian like Thomas Aquinas. Yet the Church made him a model of holiness and of simple devotion to Jesus, and that's what makes it easy for us to relate to him. We may not all become theologians or mystics or miracle workers, but we can all do what Toussaint did. As we stay close to Jesus in our days and rely on the presence of his Spirit in our hearts, each of us can walk through this world in peace and have a life-changing effect on those around us.

❧ Freedom in Christ ❧

From a homily given by the late John Cardinal O'Connor on May 2, 1999, in St. Patrick's Cathedral, New York:

Pierre Toussaint was a man who suffered a great deal. . . . It is my personal judgment, subject of course always to the authority of the Church, that if Pierre Toussaint is beatified and canonized it will be for this reason: the suffering that he accepted, the sufferings that he united with the sufferings of Christ. . . .

Pierre Toussaint's body was in a cemetery downtown, buried in the cemetery of the church that he attended every single morning for sixty-plus years. That was part of his suffering. He was black. He was a slave, and so he walked every day to church regardless of the weather—it could be bitterly cold or burning heat. The polite, respectable wealthy Catholics in their carriages en route to the same church would pass him by and never offer him a ride. That's suffering.

We had the body of Pierre Toussaint exhumed with the cooperation of the civil authorities and brought here, and he is now buried beneath this high altar with all of the bishops, archbishops, and cardinals of New York. It will be a great privilege for me to be buried in a vault in the same section with Pierre Toussaint.

Pierre Toussaint was born into slavery in 1766, only ten years before our Declaration of Independence. Fortunately it was a benign family, the Bérard family, and they brought him to New York when they came to escape the revolution led by another

Toussaint, Toussaint-L'Ouverture, in which there was much cruelty and much barbarity demonstrated. Here Pierre Toussaint took care of them rather than vice versa because he became a skilled hairdresser and very wealthy. He went out and dressed the hair of all of the wealthy women. These were Colonial days and the famous names of history would be familiar to you. The women whose hair he dressed also turned to him for advice. They saw his holiness, his insights, and the depth of his understanding. They asked his advice and they listened to it.

Because Pierre Toussaint took care of the family who "owned" him, the husband and wife, he long delayed his own marriage. . . . This was another tremendous suffering for him. He loved [Juliette] so very, very dearly and he waited so long to be married. He continued to take care of the wife of his so-called master who offered him his legal freedom, but he was not concerned about it. He knew he was a free man. They treated him very well. He did not live in slavery as we customarily think of slavery. He lived under the suffering of being legally owned by someone else, but the Bérard family was good to him and he was even better to them. So he delayed . . . to accept his freedom from the widow of the man who had originally bought him.

There was plague in New York at that time, with huge numbers of people dying. Many, many people fled town, but not Pierre Toussaint. He went evening after evening to the sickest of the sick at risk to his own life to try to help them in any way that he could. The monies that he made from hairdressing—and he did become quite wealthy—he gave to the poor, that which was left over from taking care of the lady who was "his owner." Often Pierre Toussaint was asked why he did not retire as he got older. He said, "If I retire, I would have more than enough money for myself, but I want to be able to give to the poor."

The church that Pierre Toussaint attended every day burned down. Who raised the money and donated most of the money himself but Pierre Toussaint. And yet when the celebration for the reopening came and he came to the Mass, there was no seat for him. He had to stand in the back where the blacks stood and sat if there were any seats in the back. This was suffering. But Pierre Toussaint was never, never bitter.

Sadly, there are some black people today who want nothing to do with the cause of Pierre Toussaint because they call him "Uncle Tom," because he permitted himself to be ruled by his white masters, and instead of joining in revolts against them treated them with Christian love. His answer was, "I am a Catholic. I receive the Eucharist. I receive the Divine Lord. I am not bitter toward anyone. I recognize what has been done to me. I recognize how I am treated here. But that is not enough to make me bitter any more than Christ was bitter on the cross. Indeed it was Christ who cried out, 'Father, forgive them for they know not what they do.'"

The cause of Pierre Toussaint has been officially studied in Rome. . . . Now all that remains between him and beatification and ultimate canonization will be the declaration of a true miracle. . . . We pray that that day will come and that he will be beatified.

The Life of Pierre Toussaint

1766 - Born on the Bérards' plantation, L'Artibonite, on the island of Haiti

1787 - Jean Jacques and Marie Elizabeth Bérard move to New York City, taking Pierre and his sister Rosalie with them

1789 - Jean Jacques Bérard returns to Haiti alone to handle business affairs and later dies there of pleurisy; Toussaint maintains the household of Madame Bérard, her sisters, and slaves by his wages as a hairdresser

1802 - Madame Bérard marries Gabriel Nicholas, a French planter and refugee from Haiti whose finances were ruined by the slave revolt; Toussaint continues to add to the support the household since Nicholas' earnings as a musician are meager

1807 - Marie Elizabeth Bérard-Nicholas legally gives Tousssaint his freedom before she dies on July 2

1811 - Pierre Toussaint purchases his sister Rosalie's freedom and marries Juliette Noel on August 5

1815 - Euphemia, the daughter of Toussaint's sister Rosalie, is born

1817 - Rosalie dies of tuberculosis; Pierre and Juliette adopt Euphemia

1829 - Euphemia dies of tuberculosis

1851 - Juliette dies of cancer

1853 - Pierre Toussaint dies on June 30, at the age of eighty-seven

1989 - The cause for Toussaint's canonization is formally opened, with John Cardinal O'Connor presiding at the first session of the diocesan inquiry

1990 - Toussaint's remains are transferred to the crypt in St. Patrick's Cathedral

1996 - Pope John Paul II bestows the title "Venerable" on Pierre Toussaint on December 17

God's Mysterious Designs

Saint Rose Philippine Duchesne
1769 - 1852

by Jeanne Kun

Kaskasia, Michigamea, Cahokia—strange-sounding names peppered the priest's conversation as he sat in the Duchesnes' study in France and told of his work in faraway North America. As young Philippine listened to Father Jean-Baptiste Aubert, a new desire began to burn in her heart: to be a missionary among the Native Americans. Little did she realize that it would take more than sixty years for her dream to be fulfilled. Many thwarted hopes and deferred dreams marked the long course of her life, but Rose Philippine Duchesne learned to recognize and embrace in these disappointments the plans God had for her.

Under the Shadow of a Revolution

Rose Philippine was born in 1769 into the respectable and civic-minded Duchesne family in Grenoble, in a French province bordered by the Alps. When she was eighteen, she entered the Visitation convent, Sainte-Marie-d'en-Haut. But just as Philippine was preparing to make her final vows, her father refused to give his permission because he was concerned about her future safety.

Monsieur Duchesne's fears proved well-founded as the Catholic Church became a victim of the French Revolution. While the initial aim of the 1789 revolution was to champion the rights of the "third estate," or general population of France, it soon took a violent turn. Members of the "privileged" first and second estates (clergy and aristocracy) were imprisoned, Catholic worship was banned, and church properties were confiscated. In 1792, the revolutionary government forced the Visitation sisters to close their convent. Twenty-three-year-old Philippine, disappointed that she had not taken her vows, reentered the world outside the cloister.

For the next twelve years, Philippine trod an extraordinary path. During the Reign of Terror, when countless priests and nuns were led to the guillotine, she risked her own life by caring for priests who managed to avoid capture and go into hiding. While she followed a personal routine of prayer and meditation, she also cared for the sick and dying and taught street urchins.

When the political scene began to stabilize, Philippine was able to gain the legal title to her former convent, where she tried to regroup the scattered Visitation sisters and reestablish their community life. Her efforts failed, however, and in 1804, their spiritual director suggested that Philippine and three friends apply to the Society of the Sacred Heart of Jesus.

Progressing along God's Pathways

The Society of the Sacred Heart—an order dedicated to teaching young girls—had been founded a few years earlier by Madeleine Sophie Barat. Barat had hoped to help revive Catholic life in France as the country recovered from the revolution. Mother Barat visited Philippine, who was thirty-five by this time, and accepted her and her companions into the Society, convent building and all. Thus began a devoted friendship that lasted nearly fifty years.

Though a full ten years younger than Philippine, Mother Barat did not hesitate to counsel her new sister. She recognized Philippine's headstrong impetuosity and through the influence of her friendship, sought to help the older woman become more patient and gentle.

With her years of experience and deep life of prayer, Philippine became a trusted support to Barat as the young Society expanded. She was the order's first general secretary and was placed in charge of their first convent and school in Paris. Yet all this time Philippine never lost sight of her childhood dream to be a missionary in America. For fourteen years, even though she encouraged this desire, Mother Barat kept Philippine in France, where she felt the Society most needed her strength and talents.

Then, in 1817, it seemed that Philippine's dream would finally be fulfilled. Louis Dubourg, bishop of Upper and Lower

Louisiana (an area that also encompassed Missouri), came to France seeking priests and religious to serve in his vast mission territory. Philippine fell to her knees and begged to be sent out. Finally, Mother Barat consented, and at the age of forty-nine, when many women would prefer security and comfort, Philippine threw herself into a demanding and even dangerous adventure. She was dismayed, however, by Barat's decision to appoint her "superior" of the four sisters who set sail with her, because she did not consider herself well qualified for this responsibilty.

Striking Roots in America

The story of the next twenty-three years is one of courageous steadiness and perseverance, and again of expectations thwarted and dreams deferred. After an eleven-week voyage across the Atlantic Ocean and a six-week steamboat trip up the Mississippi River, the sisters met Bishop Dubourg in St. Louis, Missouri. There he informed them, to Philippine's great disappointment, that instead of establishing a mission for Native Americans, they were to establish a school for the daughters of Missouri settlers, a work he judged more immediately crucial.

Just a few weeks after their arrival in St. Charles, Missouri, Mother Duchesne and her sisters opened the first tuition-free girls' school west of the Mississippi. They endured the hardships of rugged frontier life: a harsh climate, cramped lodgings with little privacy, frequent shortages of money and supplies, and devastating illnesses, such as cholera. But they also established schools that offered an impressive academic curriculum as well as a solid grounding in the Christian faith. The tuition from boarding schools for wealthier girls helped cover the costs of orphanages and free day schools for poorer students. This work was especially dear to Philippine because it recalled her work during the Reign of Terror when she had helped the poor of Grenoble.

Within twelve years, the sisters opened six schools in Missouri and Louisiana. They were staffed by sixty-four sisters: fourteen from Europe and fifty from the Mississippi Valley who had joined the Society. Under Mother Duchesne's leadership, the Society of the Sacred Heart had clearly taken root in American soil. Yet, blinded by her own humility, she had little sense of the success of her efforts. She often considered herself a failure, especially as superior, and repeatedly wrote to Mother Barat asking to be relieved of her office. However, many others saw things differently. Philippine was constantly praised both for her hard work and for her deep prayer life.

Although Mother Duchesne ungrudgingly embraced her role as teacher and superior, she never abandoned her dream to go to the Native Americans. Day after day, she continued to pray that God would grant her desire.

On the Banks of Sugar Creek

In 1841, when Philippine was seventy-one years old and in poor health, a Jesuit missionary named Peter De Smet proposed that the sisters start a school among the Potawatomi. The Jesuits had already converted some members of the tribe to Catholicism. From France, Mother Barat wrote to Mother Galitzin (the new superior in America who had recently replaced Philippine) and asked her to include Philippine in the mission venture. "Remember that in leaving for America, good Mother Duchesne had only this work in view," she wrote. "It was for the sake of the Indians that she felt inspired to establish the order in America. I believe it enters into the designs of God that we should profit, if possible, by the opportunity offered us." Philippine was, of course, delighted.

When the other sisters questioned the prudence of including Philippine because of her age, Father Peter Verhaegen—another Jesuit missionary—insisted: "If we have to carry her all the way on our shoulders, she is coming with us. She may not be able to do much work, but she will assure success to the mission by praying for us. Her very presence will draw down all manner of heavenly favors on the work." When the group arrived in Sugar Creek, Kansas, five hundred braves rode out in gala dress to welcome them!

Weak and ailing, Philippine could not take up the demands of teaching or even master the Potawatomi language. "If Alexander the Great wept on the shores of the ocean because he could not carry his conquest further," she wrote, "I might weep also at the thought that my advanced age prevents me from saving so many poor people." But she did what she was able to do best: She prayed. And as Father Verhaegen had prophesied, God poured out immense grace upon the mission.

Philippine spent long hours before the Blessed Sacrament in the log chapel. As she knelt before the tabernacle, lost in prayer, many of the Potawatomi would come into the church to watch her. Noiselessly they would approach her, kneel, and kiss the hem of her worn habit or the fringe of her old shawl. They were also deeply touched by her kindness as she sat with the dying to comfort them.

"The Indians had the greatest admiration for her, asked her to pray for them, and called her *Quah-Kah-Ka-num-ad*—'Woman-who-prays-always,'" wrote one of the sisters. "Everyone admitted that a great number of baptisms resulted from her prayers. Almost every Sunday afternoon three or four men or women and their families were baptized, and Mother Duchesne inscribed all their names in the register."

The Designs of God

But Philippine's joy would be short-lived. Concerned about her poor health, Bishop Peter Kenrick of St. Louis considered it unwise for her to remain in Sugar Creek. Mother Barat soon concurred and wrote to ask her "eldest daughter" to make her "greatest sacrifice" and return to Missouri.

Mother Duchesne arrived back in St. Louis on June 29, 1842, exactly a year from the day she had set out for Sugar Creek. In a letter from this time, she poignantly described her acceptance of God's plan: "I cannot put out of my mind the thought of the savages, and my ambition carries me even to the Rockies. I can only adore the designs of God, who has taken me from the thing I had so long desired."

Philippine spent ten more years at St. Charles, where she had established the first school. She remained interested in all the Society's foundations and filled her days with prayer and whatever small services she could offer: teaching a few

French-speaking students, sewing vestments for her missionary friends, mending for her community. When she died on November 18, 1852, her old friend Father Verhaegen was present to give her the last sacraments.

Mother Rose Philippine Duchesne was canonized by Pope John Paul II in 1988. The State of Missouri named her first among the women on its Pioneer Roll of Fame. The inscription on the plaque reads: "Some names must not wither." And among the Potawatomi, *Quah-Kah-Ka-num-ad* is still remembered with great fondness and reverence.

God's Mysterious Designs

From a letter Mother Philippine Duchesne wrote to Mother Sophie Barat on May 16, 1818, while on board the *Rebecca* during the voyage to New Orleans:

A storm at sea is really a terrifying sight. The roaring of the deep mingled with the crash of the tempest would drown both thunder and the booming of cannon. Add to this ear-splitting din the rolling of the vessel in the midst of great waves. The shouting of the sailors as they encourage themselves at their work has a tragic, a lugubrious effect. But their silence is even more dismal, and still worse is the sight of the captain pacing the deck in deep thought. A vessel tossed violently in an angry sea gives one some idea of the confusion of Judgment Day. The sky and the stars seem to disappear suddenly behind mountains of water. The sea, nearly black during the storm, gapes wide, revealing its bottomless depths, then suddenly closes.

The waves sweep over the deck and are hurled out to sea with a new rolling of the boat. Twice during the night the high waves burst open the portholes and flooded our berths. Then bending masts, the sails furled or torn, the steering wheel abandoned, lest the boat be too strained—all this is very terrifying unless one sees God in the storm.

The odor that permeates the whole ship is another trial, the confinement, the stench from the hold that is so nauseating and that can be avoided only by going on deck for fresh air—and one cannot always go there, especially in bad weather or when the sun is very hot. At night men sleep there; in the morning they are getting up. Besides, we cannot leave our little holes too early because people dress in the common room.

But if I have realized regretfully that many of our nuns could not endure the terrors of the sea, I have lamented still more over the great number who could not survive the stifling atmosphere of the cabins, the hard, narrow berths, the continual noise. In addition to the handling of the rigging and cordage, which often goes on at night, there is loud talking as if it were daytime. Eating and drinking go on in the common room, where two of us sleep and which adjoins the cabin occupied by the three.

Seasickness is a wretched malady, affecting both stomach and head. One is utterly good for nothing; connected thought is impossible. One can scarcely drag from one's dull heart the least little prayer of love. I could only repeat the "*Ita, Pater*," and "My God, I have left all things for you." . . . Eugenie and Marguerite were either more courageous or in better condition for the trip, for they have suffered less from this illness. For two or three days we were all so ill, we could not help each other at all, and the steward had to take care of us. Either he or the captain's boy served us tea or broth through the opened curtains. As for Father Martial, we did not see him at all those days, for he was very ill.

The Life of Rose Philippine Duchesne

1769 - Born on August 29, in Grenoble, France

1788 - Enters the Visitation convent, Sainte-Marie-d'en-Haut, in Grenoble

1792 - The Visitation convent is forced to close by the revolutionary government during the French Revolution and the sisters are dispersed

1793-1801 - Philippine undertakes charitable work in Grenoble

1801-1802 - Attempts, without success, to reestablish the Visitation convent

1804 - Mother Sophie Barat receives Philippine into the Society of the Sacred Heart of Jesus

1805-1818 - Philippine is occupied with multiple duties for the Society at Sainte-Marie-d'en-Haut and later in Paris

1817 - Bishop Louis Dubourg of Louisiana requests sisters to work in America

1818 - Philippine sets sail with four sisters on March 13 and arrives in New Orleans on May 29; opens the first free girls' school west of the Mississippi River, in St. Charles, Missouri, on September 14

1819-1840 - Expansion of the Society of the Sacred Heart in America and the establishment of additional schools throughout Missouri and Louisiana

1840-1841 - Philippine is finally permitted to step down as superior and lives as a simple member of the community in the St. Louis City House

1841-1842 - Spends one year among the Potawatomi tribe in Sugar Creek, Kansas

1842 - Returns to the Society's community in St. Charles, where she remains for the last ten years of her life

1852 - Dies peacefully among her sisters on November 18

1940 - Beatified by Pope Pius XII on May 12

1988 - Canonized by Pope John Paul II on July 3; her feast day is November 18

In the Land I Have Shown You

The Common Man's Saint

Saint John Neumann
1811 - 1860

by Jeanne Kun

What would the future hold, young John Neumann wondered as he gazed at the New York harbor from the deck of the *Europa*. The ship had just brought him across the Atlantic in a rough, forty-day voyage. Soon the Bohemian "mountain boy" would be tramping the streets of the city, searching for the residence of Bishop John Dubois, with less than a dollar left in his pocket. What a relief when the bishop welcomed him with open arms! After examining John's credentials with approval, Dubois exclaimed, "I must ordain you quickly. I need you."

Neumann had left his homeland and come to America hoping to serve the thousands of Catholic immigrants flooding the young nation in the mid-1800s. His love for his parishioners, dedication to God's will in whatever he was asked to do, and practical faith would become the foundation stones of his life in his new country.

From Bohemia to America

John Neumann was born in Prachatitz, Bohemia (now part of the Czech Republic), on March 28, 1811. His father, Philip, owned a stocking-weaving business and was a member of the town council. One of six children, John was a bright student with an avid interest in botany. His mother, Agnes, playfully dubbed him her "little bibliomaniac" because of his passion for reading.

After completing his studies at the Budweis Institute of Philosophy, John was accepted at the diocesan seminary. There he read reports describing the great need for priests among the European emigrants to America and resolved that this was God's call to him. He already knew Spanish, Italian, Greek, and Latin as well as German and Bohemian, but to prepare himself for work in the United States, he began to study English and French.

In 1834 John passed the examinations for the priesthood, but that year all ordinations were delayed because there was an excess of priests in his diocese. He waited months for responses to letters he had sent to several bishops in America offering himself as a missionary, but he received no replies. Finally, John decided to begin his journey anyway. Though he had only two hundred francs (forty dollars) to pay for the voyage from Le Havre to New York, the "bibliomaniac" bought several books to take to his mission field as he made his way across Europe saying farewell to friends and relatives.

In New York, Dubois had indeed received Neumann's letter, but the bishop's reply accepting his offer never reached him. All confusion and anxieties were cleared up when John arrived, and he was ordained on June 25, 1836. After celebrating his first Mass, he wrote this resolution in his journal: "I will pray to you, O Lord, that you may give me holiness."

Buffalo and Beyond

From 1836 to 1840 the new priest journeyed throughout the 900-square mile territory assigned to him around Buffalo and Niagara Falls, caring for three parishes and several outlying missions. John baptized the newborn and converts and visited the sick and the dying. He used any means available to reach them, walking the long miles or even riding on a cart full of manure. On one occasion, the horse his parishioners had given him ate the botanical specimens he had gathered to send home to Bohemia. John had a talent for explaining the faith in clear, simple language, and especially loved teaching children and preparing them for their First Communion.

Life on the frontier was rugged, and this was the era when many Americans were suspicious of foreigners and the "popish" faith they brought with them. Anti-Catholic sentiment flared up occasionally, fueled by the Know-Nothing party and other secret societies. Twice Neumann narrowly escaped being lynched by men who resented the Catholic immigrants and their priests.

These early years of Neumann's priesthood were satisfying but demanding. He nearly wore himself out with zeal and hard work, and he was lonely. So, when John met some German-speaking priests from the Congregation of the Most Holy Redeemer, he was attracted to their fraternal spirit. Commonly known as the Redemptorists, the order had been founded in Italy in 1732 by St. Alphonsus Liguori, and some of its members had come to America in 1832. Recognizing the priestly support they could provide him, John wrote to the American superior in 1840, asking to be received into the order. He made his profession on January 16, 1842, the first Redemptorist priest to do so in America.

Over the next several years, Neumann served in parishes in Baltimore and Pittsburgh. Much of his time was spent overseeing the building of new churches to meet the needs of the rapidly growing Catholic immigrant population of America's major cities. But his chief loves continued to be visiting parishioners in the outlying mission areas and instructing the young. Keenly interested in education, he wrote a catechism and Bible history textbook while in Pittsburgh.

Shouldering Greater Responsibilities

In 1847, Neumann was appointed superior of the ten Redemptorist foundations in America and resided at St. Alphonsus parish in Baltimore. Though he would have much rather remained a simple parish priest, he accepted his new responsibilities with the same steady faith he brought to each task he recognized as God's will. During his two years in that position, he did much to consolidate growth in the order. Around this time he also became an American citizen.

While Neumann was rector at St. Alphonsus', Francis Kenrick, the archbishop of Baltimore, chose him as his confessor. Kenrick was so impressed with the priest's humility and intellect, and above all with his faith, that he recommended him as the prime candidate to fill the office of bishop he had recently left in Philadelphia. When Neumann realized he was being considered for such an honor, he regarded himself so unqualified and unworthy that he asked the sisters in the parish convent to make a novena to "divert a disaster for the Church in America." However, Pope Pius IX was not to be deterred in his choice.

When Archbishop Kenrick received confirmation of Neumann's appointment from Rome, he went to St. Alphonsus' rectory as he usually did for confession. Discovering that Neumann was out, Kenrick left the episcopal ring and pectoral cross he himself had worn for twenty-one years as bishop of Philadelphia in his room. When John returned, he realized the significance of the cross and ring and was stricken. He immediately went down on his knees to pray—and remained there until a fellow Redemptorist found him the next morning.

Philadelphia's "Little Bishop"

When John Neumann was consecrated bishop of Philadelphia on March 28, 1852, his forty-first birthday, the diocese covered half of Pennsylvania, all of Delaware, and part of New Jersey. It included 113 parishes, with a total Catholic population of 170,000 served by 100 priests.

Neumann was sturdy and well-built, but he was only five feet two inches tall. A man with a calm, quiet disposition, he measured his words well before speaking. While the other American bishops esteemed him highly for his holiness and intellect, some of them felt he was not a commanding enough figure for Philadelphia, one of the most prestigious sees in America and a city of "high society." Many had hoped for a sophisticated and urbane man to fill the vacant bishopric; others had looked for a renowned preacher or a native-born American. However, they overlooked the fact that a large portion of the diocese was made of settlers in the regions beyond Philadelphia, people among whom Neumann was an effective and beloved pastor.

John simply ignored the opinions of those who underestimated him and gave all his energy to being Philadelphia's new bishop. Again, he handled building projects, fund-raising, and other financial concerns willingly, because he knew that if the ever-increasing number of Catholic immigrants didn't have churches, they would abandon their faith. But what he still enjoyed most was visiting the pioneer settlements of his diocese and the person-to-person contact of administering the sacraments. He even learned Gaelic so that he could hear the confessions of Irish parishioners.

One of Neumann's first actions as bishop was to organize a central board of education for his diocese. Out of his vision to have an adequate school building staffed with competent teachers in every parish grew the parochial school system that was later established all across America. By November 1853 he could write to his aging father: "Much has been done for the schools. The number of children in them has increased from five hundred to five thousand; and before another year has passed, I hope to have ten thousand children in our schools here."

In 1854 bishops throughout the world were invited to Rome by Pope Pius IX for the proclamation of the dogma of the Immaculate Conception of the Blessed Virgin Mary. During an audience with the pope, Neumann reported that he had added thirty new churches in his diocese during the thirty-four months since he had become bishop. While in Europe, he was also able to visit his family after eighteen years and finally celebrate Mass for them.

Ready to Meet Death

During the next five years, Philadelphia's bishop helped build eighty more churches, promoted parish missions and the popular Forty Hours Devotion, supported the establishment of several religious orders of sisters, championed the parochial school system, and conducted visitation tours in his extensive diocese. He also played an active part in several councils of the American bishops.

On January 5, 1860, Bishop Neumann mentioned to a friend, "I have a strange feeling today. . . . I have to go out on a little business and the fresh air will do me good." Then he added, "A man must always be ready, for death comes when and where God wills it." Several hours later the bishop, in the prime of life at forty-eight, collapsed in the street. Passersby rushed to help and carried him into a nearby house, where he died a few minutes later. As Philadelphia mourned the death of their "little bishop," word was sent to Rome: "The Church in America has suffered a great loss."

John Neumann played a significant role in firmly establishing the Catholic Church throughout the Eastern United States during the years of the nation's tremendous "growth spurt." At his beatification, Pope Paul VI said of him: "Neumann was a pioneer . . . a founder . . . one of that marvelous chain of bishops which prepared the cadre of the Catholic hierarchy in the United States and infused in it those virtues of dedication, of zeal, of efficient practicality."

But Neumann is also called the "common man's saint." His legacy lies not only in his episcopal achievements, but in the holiness and persistent faith with which he embraced God's will in every circumstance of his life. Vatican II pointed to him as a model of how every follower of Christ is to live. In 1977, the mountain boy from Bohemia who had begged God, "Give me holiness," was canonized, to date the only North American bishop to be named a saint of the Church.

The Common Man's Saint

John Neumann and fellow Redemptorist
Francis Seelos—who also served America's
immigrants—occasionally conducted parish
missions together. This is a portion of a
letter regarding missionary work written
by Father Neumann to Father Seelos
on January 30, 1850.

During the ten years which I have so far spent in the Congregation, I have arrived at this conclusion: If a missionary is sincerely and honestly motivated by a desire for the glory of God and the salvation of our German people, he will do a lot of good, but more than that, he will prevent a lot of evil. My dear Father, we ought to be persuaded of this and thank God that his arm has not been shortened. If, after a few sermons and confessions, there is no apparent improvement among the people, still they have been stopped on their way to perdition.

Even if the seed falls on good ground, it will take time to sprout, and still more time to bring forth the desired fruit. With regard to this, we are a bit childish in our viewpoint. It is as if we planted a cherry stone in a flower-pot one day, and the next we looked to see if it had sprouted or was even some inches above the ground. In this way God likes to keep us humble.

My dear Father, whenever we feel a great desire to help the most abandoned, let us be ready to go to their aid if we are sent, but in the meantime let us pray that the

Lord may help them in a more ordinary way. Since we cannot do more than pray and do penance for them, let us take things easy and leave the rest to God. . . .

Our great mistake is that we allow ourselves to be deceived by the spirit of worldly shrewdness, the desire for fame and the love of comfort. We ought to fight the temptation to make spiritual things a means of temporal advancement. Thus the things we should and could do, become for many an occasion of sin and of unfaithfulness to God. The principles of faith fade out of our hearts in proportion as we allow the principles of the world to come in. We place our confidence, not in God but in our own intelligence, experience, and so on. We seek not what is least or most difficult or most despised, but what is easiest and what redounds most to our own glory.

If only we loved God alone and from our whole heart, how easy it would be for our superiors to lead us according to the prescriptions of the rule. God would then urge us on and we would not resist. This, my dear Father, in my opinion, is the cause of all the unhappiness that seems to reign here. I believe that what is most necessary is that we should pray for one another daily with great confidence: *Spiritum rectum innova in visceribus meis. Adveniat regnum tuum* [Put a new and right spirit within me. May your kingdom come].

The Life of John Neumann

1811 - Born on March 28 in Prachatitz, Bohemia (now part of the Czech Republic), the third of the six children of Philip and Agnes Neumann

1831 - Enters the diocesan seminary in Budweis on November 1

1836 - Travels to America; ordained by Bishop John Dubois in New York on June 25

1836-1840 - Works in parishes and missions around Buffalo, New York

1840 - Applies for admission to the Redemptorists on September 4 and is vested as a novice on November 30

1842 - Makes his final profession as a Redemptorist on January 16, the first priest to do so in the United States

1847-1849 - Serves as general superior over ten Redemptorist foundations in America

1848 - Becomes a naturalized citizen on February 10

1851 - Installed as the first canonical rector of St. Alphonsus' community in Baltimore

1852 - Consecrated the fourth bishop of Philadelphia on March 28, his forty-first birthday

1860 - Dies after collapsing in the street on January 5

1963 - Beatified by Pope Paul VI on October 13

1977 - Canonized by Pope Paul VI on June 19; his feast day is January 5

A Contract of Love

Henriette Delille

1812 - 1862

by Ann Ball

Free, educated, and beautiful, Henriette Delille enjoyed the highest status possible for a black woman in a slave state before the Civil War. Yet, out of love for God, Henriette chose to exchange a life of relative ease and wealth for one of poverty and struggle. She gave up the possibilities of life with a wealthy man for a life of consecrated chastity and resolved to use her talents, her education, and all her worldly goods for the benefit of the disfranchised and downtrodden members of her race: the slaves and the poor blacks of New Orleans. Following the example of Jesus, who was himself a member of a despised and oppressed race, Henriette chose to become a servant to the slaves.

Life in New Orleans

To understand the courage and the magnitude of the choices Henriette made, it is necessary to understand a little about the social structure of the South during her lifetime, and especially of New Orleans, the city in which she lived.

As the slave market of the South, New Orleans had developed a unique social structure all its own, one influenced by the French background of many of its early settlers. During Henriette's lifetime, blacks made up fifty percent of the city's population. In addition to the slaves, there were also free blacks. Some were former slaves who had been freed by their masters or who had managed to buy their freedom; others were the children and descendants of mixed marriages. Although they were still denied many things, such as the right to vote, these free people of color could be educated and could own property—even slaves of their own.

New Orleans also had a system that came to be known as "placage," in which wealthy white men set up double households. The young women of the placage system were of mixed parentage, part French or Spanish and part black. Since it was a relatively comfortable life and their children would be legally free, many of these women were eager to adopt an alliance with a white man. Annual "Quadroon" balls were held so that these young ladies could dress in their finest and meet available young men from wealthy, high-placed families. "Available" did not necessarily mean "single," as many of these men had legitimate wives and families in addition to Quadroon concubines. Some, however, were faithful, and adopted a kind of marriage ceremony with their Quadroon "wives."

A "Contract of Love"

Henriette Delille was born in 1812, the youngest of four children of Marie Josephe Diaz, a free woman of color from a prosperous, influential Catholic family. Although the fathers of two of her siblings are known, Henriette's father has never been positively identified.

Henriette grew up with an older brother, Jean, and sister, Cecile; a second brother died in infancy. The family lived in a comfortable home in the French Quarter, and she followed the cultural traditions of her class. She received a formal education in literature, music, and dancing, and was taught poise and social graces at home. Her mother also taught her nursing skills and passed on to her a great sympathy for the sick.

In 1824, Henriette's sister Cecile met and entered into a Quadroon "marriage contract" with a wealthy Austrian man. That same year, Henriette met someone who would eventually lead her to her own contract of love, a contract between herself and God. That person was Sister St. Marthe Fontier, a French nun whose words of faith and acts of charity to her black neighbors greatly impressed Henriette and exposed her to a new dimension of love: vowed celibacy.

A Revolutionary among Her People

Sister St. Marthe's school for young girls of the free black class became the nucleus for missionary activities among New Orleans' blacks, both free and slave. In addition to the other traditional school subjects, she taught her students religion, and at night she gave instruction to adults. Under the guidance of Sister St. Marthe, Henriette became an enthusiastic lay catechist—at the tender age of fourteen! At sixteen, when most of her friends were dancing and dreaming of the ball and the men in their lives, Henriette was deeply involved in visiting the sick and the aged and in teaching black children about Jesus and the Church. Most importantly, around this time, she and a group of friends began to develop a rich prayer life, both silent and in common, at a local chapel.

From Sister St. Marthe, Henriette was inspired with the idea of an order of nuns of African descent working with members of their own race in the slave market of the country. A black nun in a slave community was a novelty. The idea of a Quadroon becoming a nun was revolutionary! Trying to pass for white was a common practice for free blacks and blacks of mixed parentage, and Henriette's family was no exception. They were not happy that Henriette, by her association with Sister St. Marthe's students, constantly proclaimed that she was in fact black.

In 1830, Henriette not only refused to deny her racial heritage, but she was also in open rebellion against the traditions of the Quadroon class. She and a few friends boldly refused to attend even a single ball or to seek the love and financial security offered by a white man. Henriette's mother worried that her daughter would squander her inheritance on the poor. To a large degree, this is exactly what happened.

Storming Heaven's Gates

In 1836, Henriette sold all her property and, with nine companions, attempted to form a religious community. But the attempt failed within a year. Most of the women disbanded, but Henriette and her friend Juliette Gaudin—another free black woman—continued to storm the gates of heaven with their prayers and their dream of a black order of nuns in New Orleans.

Their prayers were answered through Father Etienne Rousselon, a recent immigrant from France. He encouraged them to be patient. Because of conflicts between the Catholic Church and civil authorities, he felt the time was not yet ripe for the foundation of a religious order of so radical a nature. So the women waited—actively. They continued their works of charity throughout the city until 1842, when the Sisters of the Holy Family were officially formed, the only members being Henriette and Juliette. Within a year, however, Josephine Charles, another friend, joined them.

During these first years, in spite of ridicule, poverty, and hard work, the members of the little community went placidly about their work of teaching poor slave children and performing other works of charity.

Small, Quiet Growth

In 1847, Henriette legally incorporated a group of lay people of color as the Association of the Holy Family. This group purchased a lot and built a home for the elderly. Henriette and Juliette lived in this house for a time until, with the reception of a wounded man, they left its administration in other hands.

In 1850, Henriette purchased another home, using funds from loans and her own inheritance. This house was dedicated to the religious education of people of color, both slave and free. By the end of 1851, Henriette had established her small community in this house. A newspaper of the time reported that the community was "a group of pious persons who follow a community life without being bound by any vow, and of which the special object is to teach catechism to the poor and to prepare them for First Communion."

In 1852, Henriette Delille, Juliette Gaudin, and Josephine Charles took private vows dedicating their lives to the service of God, the Church, and the poor. In the presence of Archbishop Antoine Blanc and Father Rousselon, they promised to devote themselves and all their earthly means to establish an order for the education of young ladies of color and for the relief of poor, elderly blacks and orphan girls. Because of the prejudices of the times, the little community did not receive a formal religious rule of life, adopt a religious habit, or take the customary vows until seven years after Henriette's death.

Sister Mary Bernard Deggs, the order's first historian, vividly portrays these pioneer days: "Many were the times the foundresses had nothing to eat but cold hominy that had been left from some rich family's table. It is not necessary to say a word about their clothing, for it was more like Joseph's coat that was of many pieces and colors."

"I Want to Live and Die for God"

In spite of the hardships, new candidates joined the sisters in their work. Although for much of her life she suffered from chronic poor health, Henriette remained in the forefront of the group's activities, and under her direction they began to build orphanages and schools in addition to their home for the aged. At last, worn out by her work, and after a long and debilitating illness, Henriette died on November 16, 1862. Her obituary reads, in part:

> Last Monday there died one of those women whose obscure and retired life has nothing remarkable in the eyes of the world, but is full of merit before God. Miss Henriette Delille had for long years consecrated herself totally to God without reservation to the instruction of the ignorant, and principally to the slave. To perpetuate this kind of apostolate, so different yet so necessary, she had founded with the help of certain pious persons the House of the Holy Family, a house poor and little known except by the poor and the young, and which for the past ten or twelve years has produced, quietly, a considerable good which will continue.
>
> Having never heard of philanthropy, this poor maid has done more than the great philanthropists with their systems so brilliant yet so vain. Worn out by work, she died at the age of fifty years after a long and painful illness. . . . The crowd gathered for her funeral testified by its sorrow how keenly felt was the loss of her who for the love of Jesus Christ had made herself the humble servant of slaves.

Today, the Sisters of the Holy Family continue to carry out Henriette's mission of love and education to people of color in several states and in South America. Henriette once wrote in her prayer book, "I believe in God. I hope in God. I love and I want to live and die for God." She lived her faith with hope, in a life of charity. One day she may become the first native-born United States woman of African descent to be declared a Catholic saint.

A Contract of Love

These selections are from a narrative written in 1894 by Sister Mary Bernard Deggs—the community's first historian—recording the founding of the Sisters of the Holy Family in 1842 and the years of struggle that followed. Sister Deggs, most likely one of the sisters' earliest students, entered the community on May 7, 1873.

When our dear community commenced, it was very poor, but was blessed with many graces and also many crosses which are said to be the best of all other graces, as no cross, no crown. . . .

The founders were Miss Henriette Delille, Miss Juliette Gaudin, Miss Josephine Charles, and Very Rev. Etienne Rousselon. Rousselon was then vicar general to Archbishop Antoine Blanc. . . . Our dear Mother Juliette had been almost raised together with Henriette. They dearly loved each other during their whole lifetimes and had never been one week without each other. . . .

Henriette Delille and Juliette Gaudin retired to a small place on Bayou Road, and waited for some twelve to eighteen months for good Father Rousselon to build them a house on Bayou Road near St. Claude Street. They lived there and did much good work from 1842 until 1883. Many were the souls brought to God in that humble house and many a pain and sorrow did the women pass in their first ten years, but they never lost hope. . . .

We not only taught school, but also prepared children and fifty or sixty old women for their First Communion, not only for one church, but two. One was St. Mary's and the other, St. Augustine's. These girls are alive today to thank us for their being children of Christ. We are not forgotten. Since emancipation [1863], they still show us how grateful they are. . . .

Many a night did our dear sisters, after working all day, pray that some dear friend would send them a few spoonfuls of sugar. One time a servant came with a silver waiter with what one might call a grand dinner. Others sent us bundles of candles. Others came with a few pounds of coffee and others, if the weather was cold, with a wheelbarrow of wood and of nut coal. Many ladies, knowing how poor we were, often sent us old shoes or boots to wear in the yard when it rained. . . .

Our rule was well kept even in the beginning. Our first members were strikingly edifying and also very charitable; their love drew many graces. Would to God that many of our first sisters had lived some years longer to enjoy the fruit of their work, they who had toiled so hard in the beginning for the love of God. When we think how many times they worked and were obliged to wait until some rich or charitable lady sent them the cold food from her table for their meals. Would it not seem strange if our dear Lord were to refuse to grant them so many striking graces after so many sacrifices for his holy love. . . .

At another time, the girls in our boarding school became sick with measles and scarlet fever and left. Afterwards we came near starving and could not get anyone to go and see about a donation. At that time our good Father

Rousselon had gone to France. We had no bread nor anything to make bread. So we prayed to St. Leven. Just as soon as we had prayed the last word, someone rapped at the door, and there was a barrel of the best flour and rice. So we did not need anything for a long time. At another time, we were out of oil and when the prayers had been said, someone sent us a basket of olive oil and another sent two bottles. We were so thankful to God for so many graces that we say every day a prayer for them. . . .

One of the greatest pains for us after emancipation was that those owners who had previously sent their slaves to us to be instructed wished us to refuse to give them any more lessons. But that was asking too much of our sisters, for our dear Lord said, "Go and teach all nations." We, as sisters, are more obliged than others to teach all to know their God. And the day that we would refuse would be the day of sin for us, for our dear Lord said in another place that he had not come for the just, but to save sinners. This would have been preaching one thing and practicing another, for the rich have many friends when they have money. We would work in vain if we were to seek to please them and to neglect the poor, for he that is in health has no need of a doctor. ⟨⟩

The Life of Henriette Delille

1812 - Born in New Orleans, a free woman of color

1824 - Meets Sister St. Marthe Fontier, who ran a school for young girls of the free black class; soon becomes a lay catechist under Sister Fontier's guidance

1830 - Refuses to participate in the balls and other traditions of the Quadroon class

1836 - Sells her property and attempts to form a religious community with nine companions to care for the sick and dying and to catechize the uninstructed among "her people"

1842 - Henriette and her friend Juliette Gaudin form the Sisters of the Holy Family; within a year Josephine Charles joins them

1847 - Legally incorporates the lay group, the Association of the Holy Family

1850 - Purchases a house, the Hospice of the Holy Family, dedicated to the religious education of people of color, both slave and free; this house also becomes the sisters' convent

1852 - On October 15 Sisters Henriette Delille, Juliette Gaudin, and Josephine Charles pronounce their vows publicly, dedicating themselves to the service of God and promising to establish an order for the education of young ladies of color and the relief of poor, elderly blacks and orphan girls

1862 - Dies on November 16

1989 - The cause for the canonization of Henriette Delille is introduced; the Vatican reviews what is known about her and gives permission to proceed to a more serious study of her life and her virtue

The Priest in Work Clothes

Blessed Francis Seelos

1819 - 1867

by Ann Ball

ather, please pray for my daughter to die," the heart-broken woman begged her confessor. Shocked at the request, the priest's voice remained calm and soothing as he asked the woman why. After the woman talked for a few minutes, the priest realized that the child was suffering from epilepsy. "Why didn't you tell me?" he asked. She replied that the doctors had told her to keep the malady a secret and not to send the child to school.

Gently, the priest told the woman to bring her daughter to him. He took them to the altar of the Blessed Virgin, put his hands on the child's head, and blessed her. Then he told the mother that God had healed her daughter, but to keep silent about it and immediately enroll the child in school. From that point on, the seizures stopped. The girl was healed. This was but one of the many miraculous healings attributed to Blessed Francis Seelos, both during his lifetime and after his death.

"I Cannot Resist the Inner Call"

Francis Xavier Seelos was born on January 11, 1819, in Fussen, Germany. The son of a tailor, Francis was a happy, devout child who enjoyed playing pranks on friends and family alike. Three characteristics emerged during his youth—cheerfulness, gentleness, and charitableness—which remained with him throughout life. His primary biographer styled him a "cheerful ascetic."

Frau Seelos often read from the lives of the saints to her nine children, and upon learning about his famous namesake, young Francis Xavier told his mother that he too would be a missionary. Later he also told his brother Adam how sure he was that God wanted him to "go to the land which I have shown you many times . . . on the maps. . . . I cannot resist the inner call, and I will not oppose it but freely follow it."

From his early teenage years, Francis felt called to the priesthood, and through the help of his pastor he managed to obtain a scholarship. In 1842, after reading a plea to help the German immigrants in the United States, he applied for admission to the American Redemptorists. He was accepted and sent to Baltimore, Maryland, to begin his novitiate.

Being a loving person, Francis was well loved in return—by family, friends, and virtually everyone who came under his influence. He realized how difficult it would be to say good-bye, and so, while waiting for word of his acceptance by the Redemptorists, he enrolled in a seminary some distance from his home. On receiving his acceptance, instead of going home to bid his family farewell, he wrote them a tender and touching letter that didn't reach them until after his departure. In May 1844, Seelos was professed as a member of the Redemptorists, and ordained in December of the same year. In 1845 he was assigned to St. Philomena's parish in Pittsburgh.

Two Saints in One Rectory?

The pastor of St. Philomena's, John Neumann—who would someday become bishop of Philadelphia and a canonized saint—provided Seelos with an example of everything a good priest should be and do, and his witness was not lost on the young assistant. Seelos once said of him: "I was his subject, but more like a son who needed help. . . . In every respect he was a remarkable father to me."

At first Seelos had a good bit of difficulty preaching in English. After one of his first sermons, a woman remarked that she had understood very little of what he said, but added that it did her good to see him struggle so hard! In later years, however, his preaching was so outstanding that people would walk miles just to hear him.

In Pittsburgh, as in most of the young United States at this time, there was much anti-Catholic feeling, fired by radical groups such as the Know-Nothing party. On one occasion, Seelos was lured to a house by a non-Catholic who told him that his Catholic wife was very ill. Once there, the man beat the unsuspecting priest severely. Seelos never mentioned this incident, but word of the attack did make its way to some staunch Catholics in the area. They went to Seelos to convince him to have the man arrested, but Seelos would not allow it.

In 1851, Seelos was named pastor of St. Philomena's. His loving nature and faithfulness to his calling endeared him to all who knew him. His reputation for holiness began to spread, along with his wise counsel. And the healings continued. A man who could not walk once came to the rectory and asked Seelos to heal him. "My good man, I am not a doctor. I cannot cure you," the priest replied. "I am not leaving until you heal me," the man responded as he threw his crutches out the window. Impressed by the man's faith, Seelos read to him from the Bible and then blessed him. When the man was able to stand on his own, Seelos reminded him that it was God who had healed him.

A Cheerful, Zealous Heart

After nine years in Pittsburgh, Seelos was transferred to Baltimore and later to rural Cumberland, Maryland. He next spent time as a director of the Redemptorist seminary, and finally as a pastor in Annapolis. In every place he ministered, Francis Seelos was remembered for his brilliant sermons, his desire to bring people to Christ, and his kindness and consolation in the confessional. Nothing seemed to bother him. In Baltimore he was called one night to the deathbed of a young woman. Only on arrival did he realize he was in a house of prostitution. When a local newspaper found out about it, they printed an insinuating report. When Seelos' coworkers showed him the report, he said simply, "Well, I saved a soul."

At the seminary, some of the seminarians had invented a "Laughing Society." At any time, a member could be called upon to crack a joke; no one was permitted to laugh until a consultation was held by the members to judge whether the joke deserved a laugh or a grunt. If it was a laugh, everyone had to laugh and then stop laughing at a given signal. Seelos joined the society to find out what it was all about. He could easily laugh at a joke, but unfortunately he couldn't stop laughing at the signaled moment. As a result, he was sentenced to say several prayers. Within ten minutes, after having been assigned two or three rosaries, he fled the group to avoid further penalties.

In 1863, Seelos began working in the most characteristic apostolate of the Redemptorists: For three years, he conducted missions in more than a dozen states, bringing countless people to conversion. His final assignment, in 1866, was to New Orleans. Around this time, there was serious talk about making Seelos a bishop, but when he got wind of the idea, he firmly resisted it. Writing a letter to the pope, he asked to be allowed to remain a simple priest. The request was granted, and Seelos was passed over. As a fellow Redemptorist would later describe him, he was "a priest in work clothes."

New Orleans and Yellow Fever

When he arrived in New Orleans, Seelos discovered that his superior was Father John Duffy, a man who had been a novice under Seelos at the seminary. Seelos jokingly told his new rector, "Now you can have your revenge on me for all the evil I did to you many years ago." Duffy merely smiled.

Seelos threw himself into his work in New Orleans, keeping long hours in his never-ending desire to bring people to Christ. When yellow fever broke out in September 1867, he worked tirelessly among the sick and dying until he himself was stricken with the disease. During the last month of his life, Seelos remained prayerful, uncomplaining, and completely at peace.

As Seelos was dying, the doctor tried to explain his condition to him. Finally, Father Duffy told him, "The doctor says you are going to heaven." The answer was typical: "Oh, what pleasant news! How thankful I am. And to you, doctor, how much have I not to return thanks for your kindness and attention."

"Extraordinary Deeds" Not Required

Brother Louis, who had recognized the holiness of Seelos as a novice, was at his deathbed. He asked the dying priest to tell him how to please God. Seelos responded, "I think the best way is to accept the will of God, to obey faithfully and quietly the orders of one's superior, and to do the work assigned. . . . It is not necessary to accomplish extraordinary deeds."

Through the years his reputation for healing had spread. Shortly before Seelos died on October 4, 1867, Father Duffy suffered the recurrence of a crippling pain in his knee which left him unable to walk. The pain was from a childhood injury, which had been healed through the intercession of his patron saint. Duffy knew that if he had to quit his work with the sick of the city (since Seelos was already out of commission), the other priests wouldn't be able to handle the workload. With stubborn Irish defiance, he determined, "Through the merits of a saint I was cured the first time, and through the merits of another saint I will be cured a second time!"

Painfully making his way to the bedside of his dying subordinate, Duffy knelt on his good leg and prayed to God that through the merits of Father Seelos he would be able to continue his work with the sick and dying. The pain stopped immediately, and Duffy rose. But the priest by whose virtues the miracle was granted would not learn—on this side of eternity—of the miracle.

Francis Seelos' mission of healing did not end with his death. Many people, convinced of his sanctity, asked his intercession in prayer, and reports of healings began to spread. Two of the Redemptorists who had known him began to collect the reports and asked for an investigation to be opened. The ordinary process was begun in 1900, and Francis Seelos was beatified by Pope John Paul II on April 9, 2000.

The Priest in Work Clothes

From a homily given by Father Carl Hoegerl, C.Ss.R.—historian and Redemptorist archivist who worked on the cause for the beatification of Francis Seelos—in St. Louis Cathedral, New Orleans, on October 7, 2000:

We see in [Francis Seelos] a remarkable "family resemblance." He passes for one of us. He could be one of our own relatives, a member of our family; or, a close friend, with whom we need not stand on ceremony, or be in awe of. He was, as someone put it exactly, a saint in "work clothes."

Tomorrow, we're going to place his blessed remains reverently in a glorious shrine in Saint Mary of the Assumption Church, and that is the way it should be and is very fitting. But, when he hurried home on Constance Street, when he went on sick calls on Josephine Street, when he walked along Magazine Street, or came here into the cathedral, as no doubt he did on occasion, he was just one of us, a priest in work clothing.

In him the Church has put its stamp of approval on the ordinary, on the everyday, on the usual, on the expected, on the not surprising. Because that is how the life of Father Seelos was: Mass for the people, confessions frequently, sick calls day and night, wakes and funerals, weddings, baptisms, catechism instruction, homilies—all things by a priest in work clothes.

But in him there was a difference and something else. He did not let himself get bored by the usual, with the everyday.

He did his priestly duty, every day, rain or shine, easy or hard, dangerous or not: He was always in his work clothes and on the job like the faithful, hardworking priest that he was. And he did it this way—his way—because he knew that it would make him pleasing to his Lord Jesus, and help him become, in some way, a little more like him each day.

Charles Dickens, who was an avowed enemy of hypocrisy of any kind, wrote somewhere of a practice of religion that "is busy on the lip but idle in the heart." He would have found nothing to criticize in Father Seelos, because his holiness was not only busy on the lip but also, and very much so, very busy in the heart.

And that's what the Holy Father put his seal of approval on when he, as vicar of Christ, gave Father Seelos the title of Blessed Francis. His working habits made him an easy choice for the Holy Father. And this makes him an easy choice for us to take to heart as someone whom we want to imitate and be like. Let Father Seelos show us the way of leading an ordinary life in an extraordinary way. Let Blessed Seelos show us that we can be heroes without doing those things that the world calls heroic. Let Blessed Seelos teach us each day to see the divine in the very ordinary things of our lives.

The Life of Francis Seelos

1819 - Born on January 11 in Fussen, Germany, one of nine children of a devout tailor

1842 - Applies and is accepted by the American Redemptorists

1843 - Arrives in the United States and enters the Redemptorist novitiate in Baltimore, Maryland

1844 - Takes vows as a Redemptorist and is ordained a priest in Baltimore

1845 - Assigned to St. Philomena's parish in Pittsburgh, where he lives with St. John Neumann as his superior

1851 - Appointed pastor at St. Philomena's

1854 - Transferred to St. Alphonsus' parish in Baltimore as pastor

1857 - Suffers a serious illness and is forced to rest; transferred to Cumberland, Maryland

1862 - Appointed pastor of St. Mary's parish and director of the Redemptorist seminary at Annapolis

1863 - Begins preaching "home missions"

1866 - Assigned to St. Mary of the Assumption parish in New Orleans

1867 - Dies of yellow fever on October 4, a martyr to charity as he contracted the disease from nursing the sick

2000 - Beatified by Pope John Paul II in Rome on April 9

Aloha, Kamiano!

Blessed Damien Joseph de Veuster
1840 - 1889

by Jeanne Kun

On May 11, 1873, the steamer *Kilauea* deposited thirty-three-year-old Father Damien Joseph de Veuster on the landing at Molokai. Bishop Louis Maigret told the disease-ridden crowd gathered there that he had brought them "one who will be a father to you, and who loves you so much that . . . he does not hesitate to become one of you; to live and die with you."

Damien's life was to become truly a sacrifice of love as he cared for those afflicted with leprosy: The disease ultimately consumed his own body. Eighty years after Damien's death, Pope Paul VI said of him:

> Love expresses itself in giving. Saints have not only given of themselves, but they have given of themselves in the service of God and their brethren. Father Damien is certainly in that category. He lived his life of love and dedication in the most heroic yet

unassuming way. He lived for others: those whose needs were the greatest.

As a Young Missionary

Born January 3, 1840, in Tremeloo, Belgium, Joseph turned nineteen on the day he followed his elder brother August into the Congregation of the Sacred Hearts of Jesus and Mary. On October 7, 1860, as he made his vows, the young novice prostrated himself before the altar and was covered by the black funeral pall that the Congregation used for these ceremonies. Lying there under such a powerful symbol that identified him with the crucified Christ, Joseph offered himself completely to the Lord. The memory of this ceremony was to pervade his whole life.

A few years later, August—by now Father Pamphile—was among several priests chosen to work in Hawaii, but he contracted typhus and was not able to sail. Joseph, who took the name Damien when he made his religious vows, begged his superior to allow him to take his brother's place. Permission was granted.

When Damien's ship dropped anchor in Honolulu in 1864, one-third of the population of the Hawaiian Islands was Catholic, the result of the efforts of European missionaries. Since 1820, Protestants from New England had also labored among the *kanakas*—the native Hawaiians—and Christianity had been accepted by the Hawaiian monarchy.

Damien finished his studies for the priesthood and was ordained shortly after he arrived in Honolulu. He then served nine years on the Big Island of Hawaii. Robust in body and exuberant by nature, he was renowned among his parishioners for his untiring enthusiasm, his cheerfulness, and his physical strength. He was not content just to preach the gospel. He helped his people by farming and raising livestock, and he drew upon his carpentry skills to build eight chapels and churches on the island. The *kanakas* translated his name into their lilting language and fondly called him *Makna* (Father) *Kamiano*.

The "Separating Sickness"

Leprosy had afflicted Egypt, Israel, India, Greece, and Rome since ancient times. In the Middle Ages, it also spread rapidly across Europe. To protect the populace from contagion, strict laws were enacted that banned the afflicted from all social contact. There was little treatment for the disease and no hope for a cure. As a consequence, in addition to their physical sufferings, leprosy victims also bore the stigma of being "outcast" and "unclean."

By the fifteenth century, leprosy had declined in Europe, but it was carried to the New World by sailors and slaves alike. It probably came to Hawaii via trading ships that had visited Chinese ports. In 1865, at the urging of the white population who was terrified of an epidemic, King Kamehameda V issued a law of segregation. From that point on, leprosy came to be known as *Ma'i Ho'oka' awale*, the "separating sickness."

The government purchased property on the island of Molokai to establish a settlement where those afflicted with leprosy could be segregated. The site of the leprosarium, Kalawao, was on a promontory surrounded by the sea on three sides and backed on the fourth by sheer cliffs, which cut it off from the rest of the island.

The settlement plan was ill-conceived. The Board of Health officials naively envisioned a self-sustaining community, with those who were still able-bodied building shelters and farming, providing for those too ill to work as well as for themselves. When the first 141 lepers were taken to Molokai in 1866, they had no dwellings, few provisions, and no resident doctor or priest. The government had underestimated the demoralizing effects of sending the sick into exile. They felt hopeless, cut off from their loved ones, and doomed to death. "Molokai" became a dreaded word.

An Offering of Love

In April 1873, newspaper editorials in Honolulu decried the situation at the settlement. Around this time, the Catholics at Kalawao also petitioned the Vicar Apostolic of Hawaii, Louis Maigret, asking him to do more than send them a visiting priest once a year. In response, Bishop Maigret conceived a rotation plan whereby priests would relieve each other in three-month intervals.

Damien was the first to volunteer. However, within days of his arrival, having seen the desperate needs of the eight hundred exiles at Kalawao, he wrote back: "I am bent on devoting my life to the lepers. It is absolutely necessary for a priest to live here. The afflicted are coming here by the boatloads." For sixteen years, Damien threw himself into his work. He went as a priest to serve the spiritual welfare of the Catholics at Kalawao, but once he arrived, he became a father to everyone, no matter what faith they professed.

Apostle of Charity

A man of enormous activity, Damien vigorously tackled every need—spiritual and physical—that he saw. He cleaned wounds, bandaged ulcers, even amputated gangrenous limbs. When a hurricane destroyed the exiles' shabby huts, Damien petitioned the Board of Health for lumber and built three hundred houses for the sick. He laid a pipeline to a distant spring to supply water for the settlement. Previously, the dead had been thrown in a ravine or buried in graves so shallow that wild pigs ravaged the corpses. Damien dug graves, made coffins, and said funeral Masses. It is estimated that he built more than sixteen hundred coffins during his years at Molokai.

Knowing the *kanakas'* love for festivities, he organized processions for the feast days and formed a choir and band. In time, the musicians became famous as they performed a Mozart Mass for the visiting bishop and serenaded Queen Regent Liliuokalani when she visited the island. After her visit in 1881, the queen honored Father Damien with the title of Knight Commander of the Royal Order of Kalakaua.

Impetuous and energetic, Damien could also be brusque, especially when his unceasing pleas for more resources met with slow or meager responses. While he busied himself caring for the lepers and improving their situation, government officials and even his religious superiors occasionally hindered his efforts. The Hawaiian Islands were anticipating annexation by the United States, and there was virulent strife among the various parties controlling government funds. Damien never sought publicity, but when foreign newspapers acclaimed his work and organized campaigns to raise donations for Kalawao, he was derided and criticized by the Board of Health and other mission groups. They were embarrassed by the implications that one man had outdone all of them in his commitment and energy.

Damien's Congregation also feared losing government favor and at times resented the public praise he received while other priests laboring in the islands were less recognized. During most of the sixteen years Damien spent on Molokai, he was without the help of a resident doctor or companions from the Congregation of the Sacred Hearts of Jesus and Mary, though a few priests—one with a very troubled personality, another ill with elephantiasis, a third himself dying from leprosy—tried for short periods to assist him at Kalawao.

One Like His Brothers and Sisters

When he first came to Kalawao, Damien was careful to take precautions against the disease. Nevertheless, as he lived among his people, tending their sores, sharing their food, ministering the sacraments to them, and working with the same tools they did, he showed no fear of the disease or revulsion of his patients. He didn't shrink back from the call to embrace them as his own brothers and sisters.

By 1885, after eleven years at Kalawao, it was evident that Damien had contracted leprosy. In a letter he wrote to his bishop around this time, he noted:

> It is the memory of having lain under the funeral pall twenty-five years ago—the day of my vows— that led me to brave the danger of contracting this terrible disease in doing my duty here and

> trying to die more and more to myself . . . the
> more the disease advances, I find myself content
> and happy at Kalawao.

For the next five years, Damien continued to care for his fellow lepers. In 1888, Franciscan sisters came to Molokai to open an orphanage for girls. By then, Damien also had the help of two priests as well as Joseph Dutton, a lay American volunteer. Slowly, Damien's body was overcome by leprosy as his face became terribly disfigured, his larynx and lungs infected, his hands and feet encrusted with sores. Nevertheless, he persisted in his tireless activity until three weeks before his death, on April 15, 1889. A few days before he died, he said, "The work of the lepers is in good hands and I am no longer necessary, so I shall go up yonder." When those by his bedside grieved that he was leaving them orphaned, Damien replied: "Oh, no! If I have any credit with God, I'll intercede for everyone."

Damien's Legacy

It was during Damien's years at Molokai that a Norwegian doctor, Gerhard Hansen, first identified the bacillus of leprosy, Mycobacterium leprae. Today, treated with a regimen of medicines, the disease's advance in the body can be slowed and sometimes totally halted. Once daily treatment begins, the patient is no longer contagious. However, Hansen's disease, as leprosy is now called, still remains a serious illness presenting unsolved problems. The World Health Organization estimates that there are currently ten to twelve million cases of Hansen's disease worldwide.

The Scripture verse "Greater love hath no man than this, that a man lay down his life for his friends" (John 15:13) is engraved on a monument to Damien on Molokai. Damien's presence there made the world realize that those afflicted with leprosy were not "unclean outcasts," but vulnerable human beings whom God deeply loved and who were worthy of the same respect and dignity as anyone else. Damien's life of sacrifice turned attention to caring for these unfortunate men and women all around the world. Father Damien Joseph de Veuster was beatified by Pope John Paul II on June 4, 1995. The State of Hawaii has also honored him with a statue in Statuary Hall in the Rotunda of the U.S. Capitol in Washington, D.C.

⁓⟡⟐ Aloha, Kamiano! ⟐⟡⁓

From a letter Father Damien Joseph de
Veuster wrote to his brother, Father
Pamphile, in 1873, six months after
his arrival at Molokai:

God has deigned to choose your unworthy brother
to assist the poor people attacked by that terrible
malady, so often mentioned in the Gospel—leprosy.
For the last ten years this plague has been spreading in
the islands and at last the Government found itself
obliged to isolate those affected with it. Shut up in a cor-
ner of the island of Molokai, between inaccessible cliffs
and the sea, these unfortunate creatures are condemned
to perpetual exile. Out of the two thousand in all who
have been here, some eight hundred are still living, and
among them is a certain number of Catholics. A priest
was wanted; but here was a difficulty. For, as all commu-
nication was forbidden with the rest of the Islands, a
priest who should be placed here must consider himself
shut up with the lepers for the rest of his life; and Mgr.
Maigret, our Vicar Apostolic, declared that he should not
impose this sacrifice on any of us. So, remembering that
on the day of my profession I had already put myself
under a funeral pall, I offered myself to his Lordship to
meet, if he thought it well, this second death. Consequently, on May 11, a steamer landed me here, together
with a batch of fifty lepers, whom the authorities had collected in the Island of Hawaii.

I found on my arrival a little chapel dedicated to St. Philomena, but that was all. No house to shelter me. I lived a long time under the shelter of a tree, not wishing to sleep under the same roof as the lepers. Later on, the whites of Honolulu having assisted me with subscriptions, I was able to build myself a hut, sixteen feet long and ten wide, where I am now writing these lines. Well, I have been here six months, surrounded by lepers, and I have not caught the infection: I consider this shows the special protection of our Good God and the Blessed Virgin Mary.

Leprosy, as far as is known, is incurable; it seems to begin by a corruption of the blood. Discolored patches appear on the skin, especially on the cheeks; and the parts affected lose their feeling. After a time this discoloration covers the entire body; then ulcers begin to open, chiefly at the extremities. The flesh is eaten away, and gives out a fetid odor; even the breath of the leper becomes so foul that the air around is poisoned with it. I have had great difficulty in getting accustomed to such an atmosphere. One day, at a Sunday Mass, I found myself so stifled that I thought I must leave the altar to breathe a little of the outer air, but I restrained myself, thinking of our Lord when he commanded them to open the grave of Lazarus, notwithstanding Mary's words, *jam foetet* [there will be an odor]. Now my sense of smell does not cause me so much inconvenience. I enter the huts of the lepers without difficulty. Sometimes, indeed, I feel no repugnance when I hear the confessions of those near their end, whose wounds are full of maggots. Often, also, I scarce know how to administer Extreme Unction, when both hands and feet are nothing but raw wounds.

This may give you some idea of my daily work. Picture to yourself a collection of huts with eight hundred lepers. No doctor; in fact, as there is no cure, there seems no place for a doctor's skill.

Every morning, then, after my Mass, which is followed by an instruction, I go to visit the sick, half of whom are Catholics. On entering each hut, I begin by offering to hear their confession. Those who refuse this spiritual help, are not, therefore, refused temporal assistance, which is given to all without distinction. Consequently, every one, with the exception of a very few . . . , look on me as a father. As for me, I make myself a leper, to gain all to Jesus Christ. . . .

I have baptized more than a hundred persons since my arrival. A good part of these died with the white robe of baptismal grace. I have also buried a large number. The average of deaths is at least one a day. Many are so destitute that there is nothing to defray their burial expenses. They are simply wrapped in a blanket. As far as my duties allow the time, I make coffins myself for these poor people.

The Life of Damien Joseph de Veuster

1840 - Born on January 3 in Tremeloo, Belgium, the second to the last of eight children of Francis and Ann Catherine de Veuster

1859 - Enters the Congregation of the Sacred Hearts of Jesus and Mary in Louvain, Belgium, on January 3, his nineteenth birthday; begins novitiate on February 2

1860 - Pronounces his vows as a member of the Congregation at the motherhouse in Paris on October 7

1863 - Sails from Europe on October 29 aboard the *R. M. Wood* with missionary priests and sisters from his Congregation bound for the Hawaiian Islands

1864 - Arrives in Honolulu, Oahu, on March 19, the feast of St. Joseph, after a voyage of 146 days; ordained to the priesthood May 21; assigned to missionary and parish work at Puna and Kohala-Hamakua on the Big Island of Hawaii

1873 - Volunteers to serve at Kalawao leper settlement on Molokai and arrives there on May 11

1885 - Damien is clearly diagnosed with leprosy, though he was probably infected for some years before this

1889 - Dies on April 15 in his house at the Kalawao leper settlement; a Requiem Mass is celebrated on April 16 and Damien is buried under the pandanus tree where he had first slept on his arrival on Molokai

1969 - A statue of Damien is unveiled as one of the representatives of the State of Hawaii in Statuary Hall in the U.S. Captitol in Washington, D.C.

1977 - Pope Paul VI declares that Damien was of "heroic virtue," giving him the title "Venerable" on July 7

1995 - Beatified by Pope John Paul II on June 4 in Brussels, Belgium

Mother to the Immigrants

Saint Frances Xavier Cabrini

1850 - 1917

by Ann Bottenhorn

In the nineteenth century, Italy could no longer support its growing population. In the meantime, industrial expansion in the rest of Europe and in America offered a tantalizing promise of prosperity. Millions of Italians headed west. Between 1889 and 1917, Italian immigrants to the United States alone topped four million. The vast majority of these people crowded into ghettos, filled low-paying jobs, and scratched out a menial existence.

Into this desolation stepped "Mother" Frances Xavier Cabrini. She was a true mother to the immigrants, clothing and feeding orphans, tending the sick, housing and teaching the poor. Though tiny and frail, she had a large, loving heart for her countrymen, so many of whom had lost touch with God amidst their poverty. More than simply ease their physical suffering, she longed to restore their faith. "They had to come to the United States to earn a living," she said. "What breaks my heart is to see how often they think of nothing else."

In twenty-seven short years, the diminutive, frail Italian woman established sixty-seven schools, orphanages, and hospitals in eight countries in Europe and the Americas. She founded worldwide a religious order that, at her death, numbered nearly two thousand. She did it all simply by "doing the work that needs to be done." She believed absolutely that she could do all things in Christ who strengthened her (Philippians 4:13).

"I Know It Was the Holy Ghost"

As a child in Lombardy, Italy, Maria Francesca Cabrini dreamed of being a missionary to China. When she played, she filled handmade boats with flower blossom "missionaries" and dispatched them to the East. She hoped one day to follow. Sailing after her violets seemed unlikely for Francesca, however. She had been born two months early, and was delicate and infirm. The first time she mentioned being a missionary, her older sister, Rosa, replied scornfully, "You, a missionary? One so small and ignorant as you a missionary?" That was exactly what Francesca intended, and her resolve was bolstered permanently at her confirmation. "The moment I was being anointed with the sacred chrism," she confessed, "I cannot say what I felt, but I know it was the Holy Ghost."

From then on, Francesca considered that her heart belonged to Christ. She finished school, obtained a teaching

certificate, and immediately applied for admission to a religious order. She was refused. The sisters believed that
Francesca's health was too weak to stand up to religious life.
So she did what immediately presented itself. For the next
eight years, Francesca lived and helped out at home, quietly
sharing the routine chores with Rosa. Together the sisters
cared for, and eventually buried, their elderly parents. The
dream of being a missionary to China seemed to recede. Then
Francesca was asked to substitute for two weeks as the
teacher in the village school at nearby Vidardo. She did, and
two weeks stretched into two years.

Twice more, Francesca applied for admission to religious
orders, only to be refused because of her health. But by this
time, she had attracted the notice of Vidardo's parish
priest. He was about to be transferred to Codogno, and he
had a job in mind for Francesca. Codogno's orphanage was
in desperate need of reform. The two women who directed
the orphanage had proven unfit. They had received training as religious sisters, but made no pretense of living like
nuns. They made no pretense, either, of caring for the children. Francesca was asked to bring order out of the chaos
there. At first she refused, citing her desire to be a missionary
and her lack of authority over these two women. Eventually,
however, she took the opportunity at hand, and agreed to
go—again for just two weeks.

An Unlikely Entry to Religious Life

Six bleak years passed. Francesca brought cleanliness,
kindness, and a semblance of order to the orphanage. She
gathered around her a small group of devout young

women whom she trained as religious sisters. For her efforts, she was cursed and abused by the two recalcitrant administrators. Francesca had been persuaded to take their habit, to have some basis for authority in the situation, but that only made things worse. Eventually, the two nuns were excommunicated, and the orphanage was dissolved along with the "religious order" that was running it. But what was to be done about Francesca and the young women whom she had been training?

The bishop of Codogno—who knew of her desire to be a missionary—sent for Francesca. Knowing of no missionary order for women, he suggested that she start one herself. And so she did.

Almost as quickly, Francesca embarked on a determined seven-year campaign from Codogno to Rome, establishing convents along the way. She had two goals for her journey: She wanted papal approval of her order, and she wanted to open a house there from which she could direct all future operations of her sisters. In just a few short months after arriving in Rome, and against all odds, Francesca had accomplished both objectives.

Doing What Needed to Be Done

This was to be the pattern of Francesca's life. She saw what needed to be done and set out at once to do it. It was virtually her way of life: pressing forward immediately from prayer to action. Confident that what she needed would eventually be available, she refused to delay merely because it was not immediately accessible. "Don't worry," she would say with a smile. "If I were to think too much about procuring the means, the Lord would withhold his graces." She simply began with what she could do—what needed to be done—be it keeping house, teaching school, or laying bricks. The Lord supplied the rest.

Time and again, Mother Cabrini was accused of being rash. Her boldness, however, was coupled firmly to obedience. She had even obeyed, in things related to religious life, the false nuns at the orphanage in Codogno! More often, however, she obeyed the dictates of the pope, bishops, and other legitimate authorities.

After she had founded her missionary order—the Sisters of the Sacred Heart of Jesus—Mother Cabrini still wanted to go to China. However, the pope, concerned for the Italians in the New World, urged her to head west. And so west she went, never looking back.

Departing from Rome, Mother Cabrini launched her loving assault on the New World. She began in New York City, where she brought the truth of God's love and compassion for his children. She delivered this message in mostly practical ways: establishing orphanages for destitute children; opening hospitals for people unwelcome at existing institutions; founding schools that would teach the gospel as well as reading and writing.

Soon, even New York became too small to contain the love Mother Cabrini bore in her heart. She traveled to New Orleans, Newark, Scranton, Chicago, Denver, Seattle, and Los Angeles, opening schools and orphanages. When she died in 1917, she had also personally carried her work throughout Europe, and to Central and South America.

Governed by Love

It was through her work that Mother Cabrini manifested the love in her heart. "Rest?" she would exclaim. "We will have all eternity to rest. Now let us work." And the source of this love was not hidden or unattainable: It stemmed from prayer. She once wrote, "I would become weak and languid and risk losing myself if I were to occupy myself only with exterior things . . . or if I were to be without the sleep of prayer . . . in the heart of my beloved Jesus."

Her rallying cry was, "Come what may, I shall close my eyes and not lift my head from the heart of Jesus." Still, her "repose" manifested itself in activity. Love—the love she received from Jesus and the love she felt for the Lord and his people—was the power behind her work. It kept her going, and it kept her humble. "Neither science nor speculation has ever made, or ever will make, a saint," she claimed. "Better to be an idiot capable of love, because in love he will sanctify himself."

Mother Cabrini sanctified herself in love, certainly, but she was far from being an idiot. She was a shrewd, iron-willed businesswoman when she needed to be. She campaigned through each city, studying maps like a military general, walking the streets, learning the neighborhoods, contemplating trends, so that she could find the best location for a new school or orphanage. Intelligent and practical as she was, her prayer was, "Convert me, Jesus, convert me completely to yourself, for if you do not make me a saint, I will not know how to work in your vineyard and will end by betraying your interests, instead of rendering them successful."

A Witness to God's Infinite Power

It would seem that she did render many of Jesus' interests successful. Whether through dreams and visions or by ordinary begging and tramping the lengths and breadths of cities, Mother Cabrini's humility, obedience, and simplicity opened doors of compassion for countless immigrants. She was cheerful and perpetually calm. When a venture started out badly, she rejoiced, sure that it was a sign of blessings to come. "Difficulties, difficulties," she would say. "They're merely scarecrows to frighten children!" She believed absolutely that she could do all things through Christ who strengthened her. Looking back over her own life, Mother Cabrini was convinced that she wasn't even God's instrument. She was only a witness of his infinite power.

The first citizen of the United States to be declared a saint, Mother Cabrini was canonized by Pope Pius XII in 1946. Four years later he named her "Patroness of Immigrants." In 1996, on the fiftieth anniversary of her canonization, Pope John Paul II called St. Frances Xavier Cabrini "Missionary of the New Evangelization."

Mother to the Immigrants

Mother Cabrini crossed the Atlantic twenty-four times during her years as a missionary and wrote long travelogue-letters to keep in touch with her sisters throughout the world. This excerpt is from one she wrote in September 1899 while on a voyage from New York to Le Havre, France.

How sweet and good it is to go to sea, tired and drained from the work of the missions! The date had been fixed, the cabins reserved, but the second of September came upon us all too soon. During the last days I had to run from morning until night to settle certain affairs of the mission that required my attention. Night served for packing the trunks, so I boarded the ship really tired. As soon as we finished waving our handkerchiefs to bid goodbye to the sisters, rather than sitting, I fell into a lounge chair and remained there for a long time unable to move and drowsing off until I fell asleep. When I awoke, I could not believe that I was alone with Mother Virginia and then felt the whole burden of distance from you. It seemed that I still had a word to say to one sister, advice for another, and a suggestion for a third. By now, the immensity of the waters had isolated me from everyone, and the rainy weather seemed to make the thought of leaving you sadder.

However, reflecting that I was a Missionary and could not permit sadness to come near me, I withdrew into the beautiful Heart of Jesus and I saw all my sisters there. Even though

I could not speak to them, I could ask Jesus to tell each one what I had forgotten or had not had time to say. This was a welcome relief, and I regained my serenity, thinking that while Jesus inspires you to understand what I desire of you, he will also add the necessary grace and help you in exercising those virtues which must render you worthy to be true Missionaries of the Divine Heart, full of enthusiasm and truly zealous for the salvation of souls.

The harvest that God spreads before you is vast and fertile and you can roam through it zealously daily, gathering abundant sheaves. You are the fortunate spouses of Jesus, queens entitled to all the treasures of the Spouse. Be queens, then, in safeguarding the rights of the realm of your King and Lord by sharing joyfully and willingly its concerns and crosses in order to guide those entrusted to your care. Remember that those souls cost all the Blood of Jesus, so do all in your power to lead them to his Divine Heart. Labor with zeal; the power of your love will endow your actions with strength and courage. In your words, actions, and sufferings, always seek the greater glory of God. The perfection to which you must incessantly aspire must be motivated by that most noble end, the glory of God. Gather together the forces of your spirit; work, pray, offer your sorrows; sweat, sigh, and be vigilant in the constant discipline of yourself. Always hold high the banner, *Onmia possum in eo qui me confortat.* [Philippians 4:13: "I can do all things in him who strengthens me."]

Have great confidence in Jesus, and may your trust in him grow daily. You are poor creatures, but you must lean on the Creator. You are poor little ones, weak and miserable, so you must rely on Divine Omnipotence. Yes, oh daughters, lean on your Beloved, because the soul who abandons herself in the hands of Jesus in all she does, is carried in his arms. And it is in just this manner that the religious, sustained and carried by her Beloved, every hour performs many great deeds promptly and with admirable ease. The true spouse has wings on her feet and hands to work with speed and accuracy to console her beloved Jesus and to bring much glory to him with the salvation of souls.

The Life of Frances Xavier Cabrini

1850 - Born and baptized on July 15 in the Italian province of Lombardy, the youngest daughter of Agostino and Stella (née Oldini) Cabrini

1858 - Receives the Sacrament of Confirmation and experiences a special grace: "I know it was the Holy Ghost"

1871 - Begins to teach school in Vidardo

1874 - Begins her work at the House of Providence, an orphange in Codogno

1880 - Moves on November 14 with her companions into a convent building in Codogno, where they establish a diocesan congregation at the suggestion of Bishop Dominic Gelmini of Lodi

1888 - The Missionary Sisters of the Sacred Heart are granted pontifical approval by Pope Leo XIII

1889 - Embarks for the United States with six sisters on March 23; opens her first orphanage in New York City on May 3

1890 - Transfers the orphanage to West Park, New York, where the American novitiate for the Missionary Sisters of the Sacred Heart is also established

1891 - Founds New York's Columbus Hospital and a school in Panama, her first establishment in the Americas outside of the United States

1894-1908 - Travels extensively, founding schools and houses for the sisters in Argentina, Brazil, France, Spain, and England as well as throughout the United States

1909 - Naturalized as a U.S. citizen in Seattle, Washington

1917 - Dies on December 22 in the convent of the Columbus Hospital in Chicago, at the age of sixty-seven

1938 - Beatified on November 13 by Pope Pius XI

1946 - Canonized on July 7 by Pope Pius XII; her feast day is November 13

In the Land I Have Shown You

The Healing Power of Faith

Blessed André Bessette

1845 - 1937

by Ann Ball

I am only a man, just like you," Brother André Bessette reminded petitioners who came to him. Known as a miracle worker of healing during his lifetime, this humble brother of the Congregation of Holy Cross insisted on giving all the credit to God, the faith of those healed, and the intercession of St. Joseph. Quietly, he said, "I will pray for you." Time after time, healing came.

Brother André was born Alfred Bessette in 1845 in a small town near Montreal. He was the sixth of ten children, and his father worked as a carpenter and woodcutter. At his birth, Alfred was so frail that the midwife baptized him immediately. Throughout life, his health remained poor. No one would have predicted that he would live to the ripe old age of ninety-one.

"I Am Sending You a Saint"

When Alfred was only nine years old, his father was killed in an accident. A few years later, his mother died of tuberculosis. The children were all parceled out to relatives and Alfred, orphaned and nearly illiterate, was forced to find work. He apprenticed at several skills, but for health reasons, never completed any. When his parish priest introduced him to the Congregation of Holy Cross and suggested that he apply for admission, Alfred demurred at first because of his lack of education. He had never attended any school and could barely even write his own name.

But the priest persisted and even wrote his letter of application for him. "I am sending you a saint," he wrote in his letter of reference. Alfred may have lacked formal schooling, but prayer had been part of his education from his earliest days. Before his parents died, the whole family gathered every night to say the rosary, and even as a child, Alfred loved to meditate on the Passion.

Alfred's father, a carpenter himself, also introduced him to the great carpenter of Nazareth, and when he was only a child, Alfred placed himself under Joseph's special protection. Later, in his travels and his work experience, his devotion to St. Joseph the laborer, who knew both exile and poverty, deepened and took firm root in Alfred's heart. All these influences combined to form in Alfred a true love for God and a desire to serve him with his life, which did not escape the notice of his novice master.

After Alfred's novitiate, the Holy Cross superiors hesitated to admit him to final vows because of his poor health. But when the archbishop of Montreal visited, Alfred—who took the name André on entering the Congregation—overcame his typical modesty and begged for his help. The bishop told him, "Do not fear, my son, you will be allowed to make your religious profession." No doubt the bishop's intercession helped, but his novice master also pleaded his case. "If this young man becomes unable to work," he said, "he will at least be able to pray for us." Consequently, André made his profession on August 22, 1872.

The brothers taught André to read and assigned him some of the more menial tasks necessary for the upkeep of their home. André had worked at a number of unskilled jobs in Canada and the United States before he entered Holy Cross, so as a humble brother, he joyfully washed floors and windows, cleaned lamps, carried firewood, and worked as a porter and messenger—all without a single complaint.

A Contagious Inner Happiness

Brother André knew how to speak of the love of God with such intensity that he inspired hope in everyone who met him. He spoke of God as a loving Father, gave people common-sense advice, and was able to empathize with those he counseled. These traits, along with his warm sense of humor, drew people to him. "You mustn't be sad," he often said. "It is good to laugh a little." Especially with the poor and the unfortunate the good brother was merry, and his own inner happiness seemed contagious.

When Brother André was appointed doorkeeper to the order's college in Montreal, it was surely no accident. His gentle manner, his pleasant disposition, and his knack for putting people at ease—along with his ability to speak

English—made him a perfect choice. But there was more than logic here. As future events would reveal, Divine Providence was at work as well.

After his work for the day was finished, Brother André visited the sick and the elderly in their homes or in the hospital. He put all of his good nature and good humor into these outings, and some criticized him, saying he just liked to travel around in a car. But André responded, "There are some who say that it is for pleasure that I visit the sick, but after a day's work it is far from being a pleasure. Homes for the poor are filled with men and women who have been abandoned, without relatives or friends. . . . It would do healthy men good to visit the sick."

As a result of these visits, thousands of the poor, the hurt, and the unhappy came to see André in his little office. There he counseled them, cried with them, and prayed for them. At times he could be quick or sharp, especially when he was fatigued. But whenever he realized that he had spoken sharply, he would repent and remind himself, "At least they know that I am nothing but a poor sinner."

Brother André did not distinguish among those who asked for his help. He prayed for everyone. "Our Lord is our big Brother, and we are the little brothers. Consequently, we should love one another as members of the same family."

Brother André had a particular love for the Eucharist and encouraged people to go to Communion frequently. "If you ate only one meal a week," he would say, with a note of sadness in his voice, "would you survive? It is the same for your soul." Although he had a deep devotion to St. Joseph, his primary love was for the Passion of Christ, on which he often meditated. For André, Jesus' death on the cross was the supreme act of God's love for man.

Worker of Wonders and Friend of St. Joseph

After five years as doorkeeper, André's miraculous power began to manifest itself. One day, he visited a student suffering from a severe fever in the infirmary and told him, "You are in perfect health. Go outside and play." The young man did, and when a doctor came to check him, he was perfectly well. Soon afterward, a smallpox epidemic broke out at the order's college in St. Laurent. Many fell ill, and some died. Brother André volunteered to nurse the sick, and when he arrived he knelt and prayed to St. Joseph. Not another person died. Reports of these healings began to circulate throughout Montreal, and the trickle of early visitors developed into a flood of sick people seeking him out.

As a young man, André had a dream in which he saw a church in an unfamiliar setting. Later, he recognized the place as the top of beautiful Mount Royal. He became convinced that a shrine in honor of St. Joseph should be built there, but he kept his conviction quiet until the right time.

Meanwhile, the flood of sick people coming to the college had begun to disturb the parents of the students. So for a while André received the sick at a small trolley station—until the passengers began to complain. In the midst of all this turmoil, the archbishop of Montreal asked André's superior, "Will he stop this work if you order him to?" The superior testified as to his obedience. "Well then, let him alone. If the work is from God, it will continue; if not, it will crumble." When some doctors charged André with being a quack, the health authorities cleared him as "harmless."

From Porter to Construction Manager

Brother André was one of the first to count on St. Joseph as a realtor and appealed to him about property many times. For several years, Holy Cross authorities had attempted to buy land on Mount Royal, but the owners refused to sell. André, along with several other brothers and students, began planting medals of the saint on the property. Suddenly, in 1896, the owners yielded. The brothers owned the right piece of land, and André was one step closer to realizing his dream.

When André asked permission to build a small chapel to receive the sick, his request was refused. His superiors did allow him, however, to put a statue of St. Joseph in a niche on the mountain. They told him to save the alms he received and the few pennies he earned as a barber for a future project. When he had collected two hundred dollars, he was given permission to build. All he needed were laborers.

Soon afterward, a mason with a serious stomach ailment asked André for prayer. André replied by asking, "If St. Joseph cured you, would you come and work with me on the mountain? If you are willing, I shall count on you tomorrow morning." The mason obeyed, and for the first time in months was able to put in a full day's work.

The People Just Kept Coming

The first chapel was completed and blessed in 1904, and in 1908 Brother André was appointed guardian of the shrine and took up residence there. Pilgrims came by the thousands. André realized that a priest was needed, and he was given a young priest with failing eyesight to help out. After a few weeks, however, the priest told André that he couldn't see any longer and would have to quit. "I feel that I have failed you," the man said, distressed. André just whispered, "Wait until morning." The following day, the priest's eyesight improved dramatically and he was able to stay on. Pilgrims kept pouring in, and André knew that the chapel-turned-shrine would have to be expanded.

During the Great Depression, enlargement of the shrine stalled for lack of funds. Undaunted, Brother André advised, "Put a statue of St. Joseph in the middle of the building. If he wants a roof over his head, he'll get it." So a statue was brought in, and within two months construction was back on schedule. The shrine which stands there, known as St. Joseph's Oratory, today is the largest church in the world dedicated to St. Joseph. It fits André's character that throughout the entire time of its construction, he never referred to this shrine as "his" project. Instead, he said, "God chose the most ignorant one."

Brother André died peacefully in a Montreal hospital in January 1937. An estimated one million people climbed the slope of Mount Royal through rain, sleet, and snow during the seven days set aside to pay their final respects to this humble brother. Pope John Paul II beatified Brother André on May 23, 1982, and said in a homily honoring him:

> Where, then, does his unheard-of radiance, his fame among millions of people, come from? A daily crowd of sick, afflicted, poor of all kinds,

and those who were handicapped or wounded by life found in his presence, in the parlor of the college, at the oratory, a welcoming ear, comfort and faith in God, confidence in the intercession of St. Joseph, in short, the way of prayer and sacraments, and with that the hope and often manifest relief of body and soul. Do not the poor today have as much need of such love, of such hope, of such an education in prayer?

Today, many do still come to ask his help. Brother André's life inspires us who remember his words, "I am only a man just like you," to imitate his faithful service and his love of God.

The Healing Power of Faith

During the beatification process for Brother André Bessette, testimony was recorded on a total of 125 cases of healing. Here are several accounts, in the words of the witnesses:

I witnessed one of Brother André's miracles. A man was brought to the oratory, and he was tied up on a stretcher. Brother André came out of his office, looked at him, and said to those who had brought him up the hill, "Untie him and let him walk." Then, without even waiting to see the outcome, he entered the residence for his noon meal. Indeed, the man was healed, which caused quite a sensation. But Brother André had gone his way and was probably eating lunch with the rest of the community.

. . . . .

Mr. Sénécal was in his thirties, and he worked for the railway company. He had injured his leg and went to see Brother André one year after the accident. He paid several visits, but to no avail. Meanwhile his wound extended from his foot up to his knee, and surgeons decided to amputate his leg, because the bone itself had turned black from the ankle to the knee, and they couldn't do anything. Sénécal decided to wait until his novena was completed. Then he went to the hospital twice for the amputation. But since there was no room for him in the hospital, he went back home and the amputation was again postponed. Brother André then advised him that he should come and make a novena with him in his room over the original chapel. He remembered that the stench of the wound was awful, and it was late in the fall and too cold to open up the windows.

One night Brother André was invoking St. Joseph, and he prayed through the Precious Blood of Our Lord, asking that Sénécal might be healed. And all of a sudden the man felt that he was. He stood up, and as soon as the prayer was finished, started jumping up and down with joy. On the next day, a regular driver of Brother André drove the man to the hospital, so that the doctors might witness the healing. But none of them wanted to recognize Sénécal in spite of all his identity papers. They said it was absolutely impossible that such a serious wound would be healed so perfectly in so little time.

. . . . .

About 1911, on a Sunday afternoon, a young man came walking on two crutches. Both his legs dragged as he took each step. Brother André talked to him and then said, "Give me your crutches and walk!" The man obeyed. Finding himself on his legs, he became so nervous and excited that he did not even say "Thank you." He ran down the steps to the street and took the trolley car back home without a word, while people looked at him through the window.

Only a half hour later, a man came and told Brother André that his arm was paralyzed, that he could no longer use it. André told him to put his hat on his head. The man tried once, and then a second time, and then a third time.

Brother André told him, "Make a novena. You will begin by going to confession and Communion." But the man answered, "It's been twenty-five years since I stopped going to confession." "You may come and sleep in my room tonight," Brother André answered, "I'll find a priest for you." And the man did come back. He went to confession and to Communion on the next day. His paralysis disappeared. ⟞⟐⟝

The Life of André Bessette

1845 - Born and baptized on August 9 in the village of Saint-Gregoire d'Iberville, near Montreal

1863 - Emigrates to the United States, where he works for four years as a laborer

1867 - Returns to Canada and is introduced by Father André Provencal to the Congregation of Holy Cross

1870 - Enters the Holy Cross novitiate

1872 - Makes his profession as a Holy Cross brother; is appointed porter and doorkeeper at Notre Dame College, a post he fills for forty years

1896 - The Holy Cross community purchases a tract of land on Mount Royal

1904 - The first chapel to St. Joseph is built on Mount Royal

1916 - During this year alone, 435 cases of cures were recorded

1924 - The cornerstone of St. Joseph's Oratory is laid

1936 - Brother André suffers an acute attack of gastritis on December 29, followed by a stroke

1937 - Dies on January 6, the feast of the Epiphany, at the age of ninety-one

1955 - Pope Pius XII elevates St. Joseph's Oratory to a basilica

1978 - Pope Paul VI bestows the title "Venerable" on Brother André on June 12

1982 - Beatified on May 23 by Pope John Paul II

In the Land I Have Shown You

A Heart for Justice

Saint Katharine Drexel

1858 - 1955

by Patricia Mitchell

Katharine Drexel grew up in the luxury of nineteenth-century high society, the daughter of wealthy but devout parents. Along with her parents and sisters, Katharine resided in a stately home in Center City Philadelphia, summered at delightful country estates outside the city, made extensive tours of both the United States and Europe, and studied at home with the best private tutors.

At the age of thirty, however, this prayerful and business-savvy woman decided to channel her considerable wealth and talent into service for those who had been marginalized by American society: Native and African Americans. Long before the Civil Rights movement was born, "Mother Drexel" dedicated herself to overcoming the evils of racial discrimination and poverty. Her compassion for the suffering and her love for Christ had enabled her to detect those injustices before the rest of the nation awakened to them.

Beyond social justice, Mother Katharine wanted souls for Christ, whom she loved so deeply. Her interior life, centered on devotion to the Blessed Sacrament, was the fuel that enabled her to work unceasingly for her less fortunate brothers and sisters. During the last two decades of her life, after she had retired, her intense desire for a quiet contemplative life was finally realized.

A Spirit of Generosity

Katharine Mary Drexel was born on November 26, 1858; four weeks later her mother died. Katharine's older sister Elizabeth was just three years old at the time. Katharine's father, Francis A. Drexel—who presided over an international banking empire that his father had launched—remarried two years later. Emma Bouvier Drexel, the daughter of a prestigious Catholic family in Philadelphia, embraced the two girls as her own and soon gave birth to a third daughter, Louise. Tragedy struck again in 1879, when Emma—who had taught the girls to be generous—was diagnosed with cancer. For three years, Katharine nursed her stepmother through intense physical pain, and it was during this time that the idea of a religious vocation first occurred to her.

Emma's death in early 1883 revealed to Katharine the transitory nature of earthly life in a dramatic way. On a European tour in 1884, as she gazed at the beauty of the great cities, she wrote to her spiritual director, Bishop James O'Connor:

> Like the little girl who wept when she found that her doll was stuffed with sawdust and her drum was hollow, I, too, have made a horrifying discovery. . . . I have ripped both the doll and the drum open and the fact lies plainly and in all its glaring reality before me: All, all, all (there is no exception) is passing away and will pass away.

This sentiment intensified when Katharine's father died unexpectedly in 1885. Ten percent of his vast fortune was given to his favorite Catholic charities; the remaining $14 million—a staggering amount of money a century ago—was put in a trust, the annual income to be divided among the three daughters. Newspapers reported that the inheritance of each of them equaled about one thousand dollars a day.

Now Katharine was in a position to begin her own charitable works. Two missionaries approached her about the need for financial assistance to Catholic missions to the Indians. Katharine had always been interested in bringing Christ to the Native Americans, and she was moved by the dire poverty that the missionaries described. She began giving large amounts to support the building of Catholic missions and schools for them and made several visits out West to ensure that the money was being spent wisely.

"A Void in My Heart"

In the meantime, Katharine continued to wrestle with her desire for a religious vocation. Bishop O'Connor was dead set against such a decision. "You are doing more for the Indians now, than any religious, or even any religious community has ever done, or perhaps, ever could do for them in this country." He advised her to "think, pray, wait."

Katharine found the bishop's direction increasingly difficult to follow. "As far as I can read my heart, I am not happy in the world," she replied. "There is a void in my heart that only God can fill. Can God obtain full possession of my heart while I live in the world?" She longed for the contemplative life so that she could leave others to dispense her wealth while she prayed, did penance, and above all, received the Eucharist daily.

The three Drexel sisters went on another tour of Europe in 1887, during which Pope Leo XIII granted them a private audience. Katharine was trying to find an order of priests to staff the Indian missions, and she summoned the courage to plead with the pope. He responded, "Why not, my child, yourself become a missionary?"

Finally, Katharine could no longer contain the deepest desire of her heart. In November 1888, she wrote Bishop O'Connor to say that she could refuse the Lord no longer. "It appears to me, Reverend Father, that I am not obliged to submit my judgment to yours, as I have been doing for two years, for I feel so sad in doing it . . . so restless because my heart is not rested in God." The bishop capitulated. Katharine had held up "under the long and severe tests" to which he had subjected her, and he withdrew his opposition.

A New Congregation

A few months later, Bishop O'Connor suggested that Katharine establish a new order for "the Indians and colored people." Katharine was overwhelmed. "The responsibility of such a call almost crushes me, because I am so infinitely poor in the virtues necessary," she wrote. After praying for another month, however, she acceded to the bishop's suggestion. In May 1889, Katharine entered the Sisters of Mercy in Pittsburgh for formation. Her doubts accompanied her, but Bishop O'Connor assured her, "I am not surprised to find you dreading and shrinking somewhat from the responsibility of the undertaking. If you did not, I should feel very nervous about your success."

Before her profession as the first member of the Sisters of the Blessed Sacrament, Katharine lost the man who had been her constant support. In May of 1890, after a long illness, Bishop O'Connor died. A close friend of Bishop O'Connor's, Archbishop P. J. Ryan of Philadelphia, stepped in to fill the void. When Archbishop Ryan received Katharine's vows of poverty, chastity, and obedience on February 12, 1891, she added a fourth: "to be the mother and servant of the Indians and colored people."

Katharine selected a site nineteen miles outside of Philadelphia to build the motherhouse for the community, even as she mourned the unexpected death of her sister Elizabeth, who had only recently married. While the motherhouse was under construction, Mother Katharine and her thirteen new members moved to the Drexel summer home and began their training. The rule being drafted for the new community permitted daily Communion, something uncommon at that time, but a grace Katharine had deeply desired. In 1894, after extensive formation in prayer, humility, and service, nine sisters were sent to staff a school Katharine had funded as a laywoman: St. Catherine's in Santa Fe, New Mexico.

The Active Apostolate

Thus began the work that Mother Katharine would oversee for the next forty years. She crisscrossed the country numerous times—often under grueling conditions—to direct the building of missions and schools and to encourage her sisters to draw ever closer to Jesus. In her mind, Catholic education served a twofold purpose: It equipped minority children with the necessary skills to lift themselves out of poverty, and it formed their faith, bringing them Christ through the Eucharist.

From the missions in the West, Mother Katharine went south to help educate black children who were barred from attending school with white children. In Nashville, she had to use a third party to purchase an estate in a white part of town to avoid community opposition to a school for black girls. When the plans for the school were revealed, an uproar ensued. There was even an attempt to build a street through the estate to render it useless! Quietly but determinedly, Katharine continued her work, and the school opened without incident.

From the South, the congregation eventually moved north to establish schools in the urban ghettos of cities such as New York and Chicago. The eighteen thousand letters stored at the motherhouse are a testament to the business negotiations, projects, and plans that Mother Katharine undertook during those years. Busy as she was, however, Mother Katharine did not neglect the contemplative life she valued so highly. When her sisters had left the motherhouse chapel, she often remained behind with arms extended in the form of a cross, her eyes fixed on the crucifix, tears streaming down her face.

The demanding pace Mother Katharine set for herself ended in 1935, when at the age of seventy-seven, she suffered a severe heart attack. She spent the last twenty years of her life in quiet prayer and intercession. The privilege of Mass in her room was granted, and the altar at which she had received her First Communion was installed there. She died peacefully on March 3, 1955, leaving a congregation with ministries all over the country serving Native and African Americans. One of the last meditations she wrote expressed the driving force behind all her work:

> Practical conclusion: Love! Love! Let us give ourselves to real pure love. Devotion to the Sacred Heart is a devotion which alone can banish the coldness of our time. The renewal which I seek and which we all seek is a work of love and can be accomplished by love alone.

Katharine took the words of Jesus literally to "sell what you possess and give to the poor . . . and follow me" (Matthew 19:21). Faithful to her vow of poverty, Katharine wrote letters on scrap paper and drank day-old coffee to save money. At her death in 1955, Mother Katharine had used the money she inherited to establish 145 Catholic missions and twelve schools for Native Americans, and fifty schools for blacks, most of which were staffed by the congregation she founded.

Beatified in 1988, Mother Katharine Drexel was canonized by Pope John Paul II on October 1, 2000. In his homily on that occasion, the Holy Father said of her:

With great courage and confidence in God's grace, she chose to give not just her fortune but her whole life totally to the Lord. To her religious community, the Sisters of the Blessed Sacrament, she taught a spirituality based on prayerful union with the Eucharistic Lord and zealous service of the poor and the victims of racial discrimination. Her apostolate helped to bring about a growing awareness of the need to combat all forms of racism through education and social services.

Katharine Drexel is an excellent example of that practical charity and generous solidarity with the less fortunate which has long been the distinguishing mark of American Catholics. May her example help young people in particular to appreciate that no greater treasure can be found in this world than in following Christ with an undivided heart and in using generously the gifts we have received for the service of others and for the building of a more just and fraternal world.

⤜❦⤛ A Heart for Justice ⤜❦⤛

From a letter Mother Katharine Drexel wrote
after visiting her sisters at St. Michael's School
on a Navajo reservation in Arizona.

I wish I had some more days to spend with you, I much feared I failed to express the real consolation my visit was to me. Do you know it seemed like the realization of years, yes, longings of the last fifteen years? When I looked at you, the virgin mothers of the poor Navajos, my heart was full of gratitude to God because he had, beyond all expectation, fulfilled the desires he himself had given me, to do something for these poor pagans. You know God gave me this desire one or two years before I entered religion or ever dreamed that God would permit me to be a sister.

And so, on this visit I looked up in wonder at God's wonderful ways and thought how little we imagine what may be the result of listening and acting on a desire he puts into the heart. If he puts it into the heart, he will bless it, if we try to act upon it, and great will be the effect before God. It will be success before God, even if it be not so to our weak understanding. For God means that which he breathes into the soul should bring forth fruit to eternal life. God in his great condescension to my weakness has let me see with my own eyes the good results of this desire of fifteen years ago. When one is strong in the spiritual life he does not always permit this. He makes us adore without understanding.

How fifteen years ago, could I have believed that eleven of my own spiritual daughters would be amongst the Navajos and that each one of them would have a mother's heart for them.

That, God has given to you, along with big earnest desires for the salvation of your spiritual children, the Navajos. These are the desires God has placed in your hearts and great will be the effort if you continue as you do, to nourish these desires and act upon them. He will fulfill your desires with good things far beyond your expectations, especially as you have so cheerfully endured the sacrifices of the foundation of this Convent. . . . With God's help you were able to get through last winter's privations. Years ago you would not have believed you would have had the strength. Who gave you the strength? God! He will give you more strength this year.

The Life of Katharine Drexel

1858 - Born on November 26 in Philadelphia; her mother dies a month later

1860 - Her father, Frank Drexel, marries Emma Bouvier

1883 - Emma dies after a long illness; Katharine first considers religious life

1885 - Katharine's father dies; she begins contributing to the Indian missions

1887 - Meets Pope Leo XIII, who suggests that she become a missionary

1888 - Decides to become a nun; Bishop James O'Connor, her spiritual director, encourages her to establish a new order of sisters

1889 - Enters the novitiate of the Sisters of Mercy in Pittsburgh for formation

1890 - Her close friend and spiritual director, Bishop O'Connor, dies

1891 - Becomes the first professed member of her new congregation, Sisters of the Blessed Sacrament

1894 - Nine sisters are sent to staff the congregation's first school in New Mexico

1907 - The Vatican gives conditional approval to the rule of the Sisters of the Blessed Sacrament

1935 - Mother Drexel suffers a severe heart attack and retires from active leadership of the community

1955 - Dies at the motherhouse in Cornwells Heights, Pennsylvania, on March 3

1988 - Beatified by Pope John Paul II on November 20

2000 - Canonized by Pope John Paul II on October 1; her feast day is March 3

In the Land I Have Shown You

Apostle to Siberia

Walter Ciszek

1904 - 1984

by Gerald Lilore

On the morning of October 12, 1963, a plane from London landed at Idlewild Airport in New York. Among the passengers was a stocky, gray-haired man in his late fifties returning to his homeland after twenty-three years in Russia. Father Walter J. Ciszek's experiences in a Moscow prison and prison labor camps in Siberia led him to write two books, *With God in Russia* and *He Leadeth Me*, which describe the wonders that God wrought in and through him during his captivity. In these long and terrible years, Father Ciszek learned to make "the purest act of faith"—to accept God's will for him completely and rely only on the grace of God to sustain him.

I was fortunate enough to meet Father Ciszek in 1980, and became very close to him. He was a man who always had a sparkle in his blue eyes and a generous and open smile on his face. He never spoke sensationally when discussing his life experiences, but only from a point of spiritual reference. His love of Scripture was so encompassing that it became his own conversation.

Spiritual Toughness

Walter Ciszek was born on November 4, 1904, in Shenandoah, Pennsylvania. As a child, he was the bully on the block, so when he told his family that he wanted to be a priest, they couldn't believe it. Nevertheless, he entered the seminary while still a teenager and joined the Jesuits in 1928. As a seminarian, Ciszek relished physically demanding activities: swimming in a near-frozen lake, running five miles before breakfast, eating only bread and water during Lent. This would build a spiritual toughness to match the physical strength that God had already given him.

Ciszek was ordained in Rome in 1937. Although he had volunteered for the Russian missions, World War II altered his plans, and he was sent instead to a parish in Albertyn, Eastern Poland. When Poland was invaded by Russia in September 1939, Ciszek received permission from his superiors to follow the Polish refugees into Russia, hoping to be able to minister to their spiritual needs. He and a fellow Jesuit joined the Polish families in a work camp in the Ural Mountains.

However, the two priests soon realized that there were no opportunities to talk about God, let alone reveal their identities as priests. The people were too afraid of the Communist officials to discuss or practice religion. At first, the priests were tempted to become discouraged, but that's when they made an important discovery: Their sole purpose in being there was to do the will of God, not as they wished it to be, but as God envisioned it. As Ciszek later wrote:

> God's will for us was the twenty-four hours of each day: the people, the places, the circumstances he set before us in that time. Those were the things God knew were important to him and to us at that moment, and those were the things upon which he wanted us to act, not out of any abstract principle or out of any subjective desire to "do the will of God." No, these things, the twenty-four hours of this day, were his will; we had to learn to recognize his will in the reality of the situation and act accordingly. We had to learn to look at our daily lives, at everything that crossed our path each day, with the eyes of God . . . recognizing that he had a goal and a purpose in bringing us into contact with these things and these people, and striving always to do that will—his will—every hour of every day in the situations in which he had placed us.

A Moment of Conversion

When Germany invaded Russia in June 1941, Ciszek was arrested by the Russian secret police, along with hundreds of others who were suspected of spying. Without a trial, he was convicted of being a "Vatican spy" and spent the next five years in solitary confinement in the dreaded Lubianka Prison in Moscow.

His stark and empty cell measured only six feet by ten feet, with white walls and ceiling. A constantly lit bare bulb hung from the ceiling. The one window was completely barred and shuttered so that only a little strip of sky could be seen at the top. The cell held nothing else but a bed and a toilet bucket with a lid. Sleeping was allowed only at night. During his time here, Ciszek was subjected to the most prolonged and intense interrogation sessions.

These years in Lubianka were a turning point in Ciszek's life. At first, he saw the interrogations as a contest of wills, but they gradually wore him down. After the first year, he signed a false statement admitting to espionage, which earned him a fifteen-year sentence of hard labor. Finally, "the blackness" closed in around him. He felt utter failure and despair. He realized he had lost sight of the Lord. Recognizing that he had to seek God immediately, he turned to him in prayer.

It was a moment of conversion. From that point on, Ciszek was able to live in a spirit of self-abandonment to God. With an attitude of total trust and absolute faith, he viewed all of life's situations as a gift from the hand of God. Previously, he had trusted God and had cooperated with his grace—but only to a degree. "Only when I had reached a point of total bankruptcy of my own powers had I at last surrendered," he wrote in *He Leadeth Me*.

Although he prayed constantly, Ciszek realized that in the beginning, he had prayed for the wrong things. Gradually, he learned to free his prayer of self-seeking and instead offer his suffering in intercession on behalf of those suffering in the world. He gave up worrying about what tomorrow would bring and sought only God's will. God's will was not *in* the situation or circumstances, but actually *was* the situation itself, as it occurred moment by moment. His duty was to respond in Christ's spirit of love, forgiveness, and compassion.

A Thriving Prison Parish

In June 1946, Father Ciszek was released from Lubianka to serve out the remainder of his sentence doing hard labor in far off Arctic Siberia. A long journey in a railroad car and river tug ended in the prison camp of Dudinka, near Norilsk. There he worked as a coal heaver, among hard criminals, in the bitter Siberian weather. Sometimes the temperatures dropped to thirty degrees below zero—even in October.

Ciszek was assigned to a variety of jobs, all of them dangerous and exhausting. He was sent to blast lumber out of the frozen river. When the huge logs, three feet thick and thirty feet long, floated to the top of the icy water, prisoners were sent out with poles to pull them in. He worked in the mines and in a copper-smelting factory and put up buildings in the city of Norilsk. Food was scarce, living conditions abominable, and clothing minimal. The prisoners were chronically undernourished, overworked, and nearly dead from the unrelenting cold.

However, Father Ciszek's spiritual work with the other prisoners was so productive that he could describe the result as a "thriving parish." Under the pretext of going for a walk with fellow prisoners, he heard confessions. He said secret Masses in the barracks. At various spots in the camp, he would meet with men in groups of twos and threes to distribute Communion. He delivered sermons "walking up and down in a group in the yard."

On the Road to Freedom

In 1953, news of Stalin's death was broadcast over the camp's loudspeakers. In camp after camp, revolts broke out and lasted for months until the Soviet Army put them down through bloody intervention. Prisoners were divided and sent to different work sites. Ciszek went first to the stone quarries, then to the coal mines, where the constant danger of cave-ins was especially nerve-racking. His health soon deteriorated, and the doctor in the medical center told him that he would not survive unless he left the mines. By this time, his sentence had nearly come to an end, and in April of 1955, he was finally set free after having served all but three months of his fifteen-year sentence.

As a convicted "spy," Ciszek was not free to leave Russia, and he could not live wherever he chose. He spent his first three years in Norilsk, but his priestly services were in such demand that the KGB ordered him to leave. The same thing happened in the next town that he lived in, until he was forced to move again. In the meantime, he was able to get a letter—for the first time—to his sisters in the United States.

In September 1963, Ciszek was called from his job as an auto mechanic to meet a member of the KGB. This began a mystifying procedure that ended in a Moscow airport. Only at the last moment did Father Ciszek understand that he and another American citizen were being sent back to the United States in exchange for two Soviet agents who had been arrested in the United States.

God as the Great Puzzle Master

Rather than become embittered or view his years in Russia as a waste, Walter Ciszek had a clear and strong sense of the meaning of his life. In all his pain and frustration, he came to understand that the oppressive circumstances were in fact God's will for him at that time. As the Great Puzzle Master, God had been at work, communicating his vision to a soul open and willing to listen—a soul slowly learning to let go and to let his Father in heaven take over the assembling of the pieces.

When asked how he survived, Father Ciszek would always reply in the same way. It was simply "God's Providence." But it was only gradually that he came to appreciate the truths about God's care. After much anguish of soul and a great deal of prayerful reflection, these truths sustained him through the long years of darkness and suffering. "God is a very patient teacher, and I was a most stubborn pupil," he said.

Father Ciszek continued his priestly work in the John XXIII Center at Fordham University—now known as the Center for Eastern Christian Studies and located at the University of Scranton in Pennsylvania—by giving retreats, talks, and counseling to many people who came to see him. During the last eight years of his life, he suffered from a severe heart condition, emphysema, and arthritis. He died peacefully in his sleep on the feast of the Immaculate Conception, December 8, 1984.

Saints are people who truly become one with God, accept what he has chosen for them, and live entirely in the moment. God's plan for Father Ciszek's life continues to unfold. Almost immediately after his death, a petition to recognize his heroic virtues and outstanding holiness was circulated by Mother Marjia, the superior of Holy Annunciation Monastery, a Byzantine Carmelite community which Ciszek helped found. All information, sworn testimonies, and published and unpublished material gathered regarding him are currently being prepared and forwarded by the Diocese of Allentown, Pennsylvania, to the Congregation for the Causes of Saints in Rome. If his heavenly Father so desires, Father Walter Ciszek will one day be canonized.

Apostle to Siberia

After Father Walter Ciszek returned to
America, he realized that, through long years
of isolation and suffering in the Soviet Union,
God had led him to "an understanding of
life and his love that only those who have
experienced it can fathom." In 1972, he
wrote *He Leadeth Me* with the hope of
helping others to "understand these
truths a little better." This selection
is from that book.

I sat in the train headed for Norilsk, exhilarated by my new
freedom, and yet thinking such thoughts. What did it
mean for me to be free, for any man to be free? I was out
of the prison camps and free from the rigorous daily order, free
to order my own life, free to make each day's decisions for
myself. In that sense I was free, yet I was not free of all restrictions. There were certain restrictions on me especially as an
ex-prisoner, there would always be special restrictions on me
as long as I carried the *polozenie pasporta*. Yet these restrictions
differed only in detail from the restrictions that bind every
man in every society: the rules and observances, laws and customs, even the "accepted" traditions of family, church, society, or culture. No man's freedom is absolute.

Ultimately, the only absolute freedom we have
resides in a man's free will. And that freedom was given
us by our Creator, essentially so that we might freely
choose to love and serve him. All other creatures serve

him out of exigency; by their very being and existence they witness to his power and his love, or reflect his glory and beauty in some way. Only to man and the angels has he given the power of freely choosing to love and serve him. He has made us a little less than the angels, has given us intellect and free will—and that is the hallmark of man, at once his crowning glory, his most precious gift, his most terrifying responsibility. Only man can freely choose not to serve his Creator.

It is in choosing to serve God, to do his will, that man achieves his highest and fullest freedom. It may seem paradoxical to say that our highest and fullest freedom comes when we follow to the least detail the will of another, but it is true nonetheless when that other is God. I could testify from my own experiences, especially from my darkest hours in Lubianka, that the greatest sense of freedom, along with peace of soul and an abiding sense of security, comes when a man totally abandons his own will in order to follow the will of God. Never again could I doubt that the greatest assurance I could have in my life came from knowingly and willingly following God's will as manifested to me. I knew only too well how shallow and unsafe it was for me to follow my own will, my own inclinations and desires, unless they were in conformity to his. I realized then, and I felt it more deeply each day, that true freedom meant nothing else than letting God operate within my soul without interference, giving preference to God's will as manifested in the promptings, inspirations, and other means he chose to communciate, rather than in acting on my own initiatives.

For those who do not believe in God, I suppose, such thoughts will seem sheer nonsense or unexplainable stupidity. For me, however, there could be no doubt: the fullest freedom I had ever known, the greatest sense of security, came from abandoning my will to do only the will of God. What was there to fear so long as I did his will? Not death. Not failure, except the failure to do his will. "For if God is with us, who can stand against us?" Choosing to do his will and experiencing the spiritual freedom that followed was my greatest joy and the source of tremendous interior strength. For to know that he directed me in all my actions, that he sustained me with his grace, gave me a sense of peace and courage beyond description. Even in moments of human discouragement, the consciousness that I was fulfilling God's will in all that happened to me would serve to dispel all doubt and desolation. Whatever the trials of the moment, whatever the hardships or sufferings, more important than all these was the knowledge that they had been sent by God and served his divine providence. I could not always fathom the depths of his providence or pretend to understand his wisdom, but I was secure in the knowledge that by abandoning myself to his will I was doing as perfectly as I could his will for me.

The Life of Walter Ciszek

1904 - Born on November 4 in Shenandoah, Pennsylvania, of Polish immigrant parents

1928 - Enters the Jesuit novitiate in Poughkeepsie, New York, on September 7

1930 - Writes a letter to the Jesuit superior general, offering himself in response to Pope Pius XI's request for Jesuits to prepare for missionary work in Russia

1937 - Completes his studies at Gregorian University and the Russicum (Russian College) in Rome and is ordained in the Russian Rite on June 24

1938 - Teaches ethics to Jesuit seminarians in Albertyn, Poland, and serves as "a horse-and-buggy priest" among Russian immigrants there

1939 - Hitler invades Poland on September 1; Russia occupies Albertyn on October 17

1940 - Father Ciszek enters Russia with the permission of his superiors to work among Polish Catholic refugees in Chusovoy in the Ural Mountains

1941 - Arrested on June 22 by the Russian secret police and later transported to Lubianka prison in Moscow, where he undergoes frequent interrogation

1942 - Convicted as a "Vatican spy" and sentenced on July 26 to fifteen years of hard labor in Arctic Siberia, but is held at Lubianka for four more years

1946 - Sent to serve out the remainder of his sentence at various labor camps in Siberia

1947 - Jesuits in New York celebrate a memorial Mass for Father Ciszek, missing in the Soviet Union for seven years and presumed dead

1955 - Father Ciszek is set free from the labor camp on April 22, but as a convicted "spy" is required to remain in Norilsk, where he works at a chemical factory and resumes ministry as a priest; during this time receives permission from the police to write to his sisters in America

1958 - Banned from continuing to serve as a priest in Norilsk and sent to Krasnoyarsk, where he again starts a parish; banned from Krasnoyarsk and gets a job as an auto mechanic in Abakan, where he remains for four years

1963 - Summoned to Moscow to be exchanged for a Soviet agent who was arrested in the United States; arrives at New York's Idlewild Airport on October 12 after twenty-three years in the Soviet Union

1964 - *With God in Russia,* Father Ciszek's account of his years in the Soviet Union, is published

1972 - Completes his second book, *He Leadeth Me*, on the spiritual truths that sustained him throughout his experiences

1984 - Dies on December 8, the feast of the Immaculate Conception, at the age of eighty

Sources and Acknowledgments

*Every effort has been made to locate and secure permission
for the inclusion of all copyrighted material in this book. If any
such acknowledgments have been inadvertently omitted,
the publisher would appreciate receiving full information
so that proper credit may be given in future editions.*

Page 17   From "The Jogues Papers," translated and arranged,
with a memoir by John Gilmary Shea, *Collections
of the New York Historical Society*, Second Series,
Volume III, D. Appleton and Company,
New York, 1857.

Page 31   From *The Writings of Marguerite Bourgeoys:
Autobiography and Spiritual Testament*, translated from
the French by Sister Mary Virginia Cotter, C.N.D.,
Congregation de Notre Dame, Montreal, 1976.
Used by permission.

Page 45   From *Kino's Historical Memoir of Pimería Alta*
(originally titled *Celestial Favors of Jesus, Most Holy
Mary, and the Most Glorious Apostle of the Indies, San
Francisco Xavier*), by Eusebio Francisco Kino, S.J.,
translated and annotated by Herbert Bolton,
University of California Press, Berkeley and Los
Angeles, 1948. (Re-publication of 1919 edition by
Arthur Clark Co., Cleveland.)

Page 59   The Litany of Kateri Tekakwitha and other
information concerning her is available at the Web
site: http://www.bluecloud.org/29.html

Page 70   From *Four Metaphors: Ground of Grey Nun Spirituality,* by Lowell Glendon, S.S. © 2001 by Grey Nuns of the Sacred Heart. Used by permission. Additional information is available at the Web site: http://www.greynun.org.

Page 83   From *Mrs. Seton,* by Joseph I. Dirvin, C.M. © 1962 by Farrar, Straus & Cudahy Inc. Copyright renewed © 1990 by Farrar, Straus & Giroux, Inc. Reprinted by permission of Farrar, Straus and Giroux, LLC.

Page 97   From a homily given by John Cardinal O'Connor in St. Patrick's Cathedral, New York, on May 2, 1999. Used by permission from *Catholic New York.* The entire text of this homily can be found at the Web site: http://www.cny.org/archive/ch/ch050699.htm.

Page 111   From *Philippine Duchesne: Frontier Missionary of the Sacred Heart,* by Louise Callan, R.S.C.J., The Newman Press, Westminster, Maryland, 1965. Copyright © 1965 by the Missionary Society of St. Paul the Apostle in the State of New York.

Page 125   From *Venerable John Neumann, C.Ss.R.: Fourth Bishop of Philadelphia,* by Michael J. Curley, C.Ss.R., The Catholic University of America Press, Washington, D.C., © 1952 by the Redemptorist Fathers of the Baltimore Province. Used by permission.

Page 193   From *Brother André According to Witnesses*, by
            Bernard LaFreniere, C.S.C. Seven Lectures to the
            Brothers of Holy Cross in Austin, Texas. © by St.
            Joseph's Oratory, Montreal, Canada. Used by
            permission.

Page 207   From *Katharine Drexel: A Biography*, by Sister
            Consuela Marie Duffy, S.B.S. © 1966 by The Sisters
            of the Blessed Sacrament. Used by permission.

Page 221   From *He Leadeth Me*, by Walter J. Ciszek, S.J.,
            with Daniel Flaherty, S.J., Ignatius Press, San
            Francisco, 1995. © 1973 by Walter J. Ciszek.
            Used by permission.

In the Land I Have Shown You

Also in this Series. . .

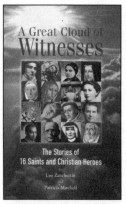

A Great Cloud of Witnesses
Includes Sts. Francis Xavier, Catherine of Siena, Bernard of Clairvaux, Bernadette Soubirous, John Bosco and more!
Item # BCLOW8

I Have Called You by Name
Includes Sts. Thérèse of Lisieux, Teresa of Avila, Augustine, Ignatius of Loyola, Joan of Arc, Thomas Becket and more!
Item # BCLOW9

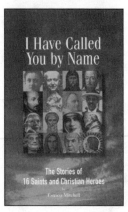

Both books feature practical and inspiring biographies of sixteen saints and heroes of the faith. Each book softcover, 5 x 8, 216 pages

"The glimpses into the lives of these witnesses for Christ draw us closer to them and make us realize that we, too, can 'fight the good fight' and 'run with perseverance the race' that God has set before us."
—Ann Ball,
author of *Faces of Holiness*